Buttons, Bones,

and the

Organ-Grinder's Monkey

Buttons, Bones, and the Organ-Grinder's Monkey

Tales of Historical Archaeology

by Meg Greene

Linnet Books
North Haven, Connecticut

First published 2001 as a Linnet Book,

an imprint of The Shoe String Press, Inc.,

2 Linsley Street, North Haven, Connecticut 06473.

www.shoestringpress.com

Library of Congress Cataloging-in-Publication Data

Greene, Meg.

   Buttons, bones, and the organ-grinder's monkey : tales of historical archaeology / by
Meg Greene.

      p. cm.

   Includes bibliographical references and index.

   ISBN 0-208-02498-0 (lib. bdg. : alk. paper)

   1. Archaeology and history—Juvenile literature. 2. Excavations
(Archaeology)—Juvenile literature. 3. Archaeology and history—United States—Juvenile
literature. 4. United States—Antiquities—Juvenile literature. [1. Archaeology and history.
2. Excavations (Archaeology) 3. United States—Antiquities.] I. Title.

CC77.H5 G74 2001

973—dc21   00-069428

The paper in this publication meets the minimum requirements of American National
Standard for Information Sciences—Permanence of Paper for Printed Library Materials,
ANSI Z39.48—1984. ∞

Designed by Nancy-jo Funaro

Printed in the United States of America

To my father and mother

Contents

Acknowledgments

Rarely is a complete book the work of a single person, and this book is no different. I would like to thank the following persons and institutions for their help:

The Association for the Preservation of Virginia Antiquities, and Michael Lavin at Jamestown; the Texas Historical Commission; The Thomas Jefferson Memorial Foundation; Kitty Belle Deernose, Museum Curator at the Little Bighorn Battlefield National Monument; the Denver Public Library; Dr. Rebecca Yamin of John Milner Associates, Inc., for her time, patience, and suggestions with the Five Points chapter; Diantha Thorpe of The Shoe String Press and Deborah Kops who helped bring the manuscript to life; and my husband Mark, whose patience and encouragement helped bring the book to life.

Any mistakes or incorrect information are my own.

Introduction
Time Detectives*

For archaeologists the truth is never on the surface. It lies buried in the dirt, the trash pit, and even beneath the sea. Every day we discard items for which we no longer have any use: chipped dishes, aluminum cans, glass bottles, cellophane wrappers, paper boxes, plastic bags, and sometimes old clothing. Rarely do we give much thought to the objects we toss into the garbage. After they have served their purpose, we just want to be rid of them.

Yet studying the broken bottles and plates, the remnants of buttons and bones, and the fragments of carpet and clothing that men and women left behind is often more revealing than we might at first suppose. From these remains of everyday life, archaeologists can learn a great deal about how ordinary people lived and worked, ate and slept, played and fought. New technologies, such as the magnetometer sensor, an instrument that detects the presence of metal, and the cofferdam, a watertight enclosure that is lowered into the ocean, have aided archaeologists in these efforts. When exploring a site, though, archaeologists still rely on methods pioneered more than two hundred years ago.

The chapters that follow examine the techniques and the contributions of a particular kind of archaeology known as "historical archaeology."

---

*From *Time Detectives: How Archaeologists Use Technology to Recapture the Past* by Brian Fagan.

Unlike traditional archaeologists, who only study the material remains of people who lived long ago, historical archaeologists depend on the written record to help interpret their finds. They may consult official documents and other published sources, such as maps and city directories, as well as private letters and diaries. It may help to think of historical archaeologists as "time detectives" who piece together strands of evidence from various sources in an attempt to bring the mysteries of the past into clearer focus.

Today, those interested in understanding the past make a point of studying not only the deeds of famous people but also the lives of ordinary folk, including Native Americans, slaves, and immigrants, whose place in history has been neglected or forgotten. For a long time, scholars assumed that they could not learn very much about these people. They complained that most of them had at best left behind only sparse written records; many could not read or write at all. Conventional wisdom suggested there was very little that even the most enterprising and imaginative historian could do to reconstruct their lives.

Historical archaeologists defied conventional wisdom. Their approach to studying the past allowed them to see that these ordinary Americans had, in fact, left behind all sorts of interesting and important "documents" that more than made up for the lack of written sources. These tireless researchers showed that a broken china teacup, a torn piece of fabric, a tarnished ring, or a pair of old boots may each in its own way contribute as much to understanding the past as the Declaration of Independence or the Emancipation Proclamation. Every "document," of course, reveals a slightly different aspect of the past. By itself, no single piece of evidence is ever complete. But all artifacts have their own story to tell and each story deepens our knowledge about those who came before us.

In the five episodes in historical archaeology that make up this book, time detectives have gathered new information to shed new light on historical mysteries that have puzzled us for a long time. Some of these episodes do treat well-known historical figures such as Thomas Jefferson and George Armstrong Custer, and famous places such as Virginia's Jamestown. Each chapter, however, explains how historical archaeologists have gone beyond the familiar to reveal the most extraordinary history hidden in the most ordinary artifacts. Their discoveries may sometimes confirm what we already suspected about the life of a person or the history of an event. More often, they force us to question our assumptions and rethink our conclusions. Historical archaeologists have combined painstaking labor and careful research with imaginative analysis to bring the past to life. Through discarded objects they have recovered, they have allowed it to speak to us.

I.

Mystery, Murder, and Mud: The Discovery of the Jamestown Fort

"A verie fit place for the erecting of a great cittie."
—Captain John Smith, 1608

Jamestown, Virginia is different. As the first permanent English settlement in North America, Jamestown certainly is an important part of our past. As one archaeologist stated: "This is the birthplace, the absolute cradle of everything we know as America."[1]

Given its uncontested significance, scholars naturally tried to learn all they could about the founding, operation, and eventual decline of the Jamestown settlement. In time, they amassed a great deal of information, but serious gaps in their knowledge remained. Historians and archaeologists, for example, generally dismissed the idea that any trace of the Jamestown fort existed. Surely the fort, built by the 105 English settlers who arrived at the lonely outpost in 1607, had washed away into the James River. But had it? Archaeologist William Kelso didn't think so. He was certain that the remains of fort had survived, although neither he nor anyone else knew exactly where to look for them.

In 1963, while he was a graduate student in history at the College of William and Mary in nearby Williamsburg, Virginia, Kelso had listened intently as a National Park Service ranger explained to visitors about the demise and disappearance of the Jamestown fort. Kelso was skeptical, for he did not believe that the fort had been washed away by the James River as many believed. Long before his visit to Jamestown, Kelso had been intrigued by the site. As an undergraduate, he had seen an aerial photograph of the archaeological excavations carried on in 1957 and tried to imagine, as he put it, "digging in that 'ancient' Jamestown soil with my own hands."[2]

The park ranger's explanation of what had happened to the fort did not convince him. Long before he became a professional archaeologist, Kelso found himself questioning the conventional wisdom about Jamestown. Why, he wondered, would the settlers, many of whom were professional soldiers, build a fort on unstable and dangerous marshes? He later recalled that:

> I naively asked a park ranger where the old fort site was. I was surprised when he pointed to a lone cypress tree growing way off shore and said, "Unfortunately out there and lost for good." Confused, I looked back . . . and asked again but what about here? He thought for a moment and then replied with a shrug of his shoulders which I took as a "maybe."[3]

Little did Kelso realize that near the very spot toward which he had pointed lay the answer to an age-old mystery. Thirty years passed before he found out he had been right.[4]

Eastern Virginia, 1607
"A Place You May Perchance to Find"

Their orders were explicit: "Do your best Endeavor to find a Safe port in the Entrance of Some navigable river. . . . A place you may perchance to find a hundred miles from the Rivers mouth."[5] So saying, the Council of Virginia, the governing body of the Virginia Company of London, dispatched three ships, the *Susan Constant*, the *Godspeed*, and the *Discovery*, and 144 men with instructions to establish the first permanent English settlement in North America.

The wayfarers came from all walks of life. One was Captain John Smith, who later helped save the Jamestown settlement from failure, and who became famous for his relationship with the Indian princess

Pocahontas. There were other "gentlemen" (noblemen and soldiers), a minister of the Church of England, a "chirugeon" (surgeon/doctor), several carpenters, blacksmiths and laborers, a tailor, and four boys. For some, coming to the New World represented the opportunity to make a new beginning. By the end of the sixteenth century, in fact, the British government had begun to encourage emigration. Between 1500 and 1650, the population of England had grown from 3 million to 4.5 million, an increase of 50 percent. As a result, poverty, famine, overcrowding, and unemployment had become rampant in late sixteenth-century England. Along with theft and violence, the mass of idle, hungry poor threatened peace and stability, and government policies toward them were harsh. Thoughtful men saw an obvious and, they thought, humane solution: get the poor out of England by sending them to the New World. There, English officials hoped, the poor would find limitless opportunities for work and boundless possibilities for upward social mobility. They could improve their lives and, at the same time, enrich the mother country.

Others, though, came to the New World not to escape poverty but to get rich. A number of the passengers, who listed themselves as "gentlemen," were the sons of aristocratic families that could not provide for their future welfare. According to the English law of primogeniture, which means "first-born," the eldest son inherited all of the family property upon the death of his father. His younger brothers had to content themselves with careers in the church or the military, since the odds were against their ever gaining control of the family estate. By the late sixteenth and early seventeenth centuries, however, English overseas exploration presented these disinherited aristocrats with another option. They could journey to the New World in the hope of acquiring the property and fortune that the laws of England had denied them.

In 1606, therefore, these noblemen, joined by a group of London merchants, had petitioned King James I for permission to found an English colony in the New World. The king granted them a charter, allowing them to form two companies: the Virginia Company of London and the Virginia Company of Plymouth. On a cold, gray Saturday in December 1606, the colonists set sail. Four months later, on April 26, 1607, lookouts aboard the *Susan Constant*, the *Godspeed*, and the *Discovery* sighted land. Crossing the Chesapeake Bay, the vessels soon arrived at the mouth of a large river that the Englishmen called the James in honor of their king. On May 12, the captain of the expedition, Christopher Newport, signaled the ships to anchor off a small island. Their location was thirty-six miles upriver from the mouth of the Chesapeake Bay, instead of the hundred miles as recommended by the Council of Virginia. Already the newly arrived Englishmen had begun to disregard their orders.[6]

Newport had good reasons for making this choice. The proposed site had a deep-water channel that allowed for the mooring of ships close to land. This made it easier to guard the ships and also made it difficult for enemy ships, especially those of the Spanish, to surprise the English settlers. Hidden from view by another island, which the English called Hog Island, the site could not be easily detected. Connected to the mainland on one side by a small isthmus (a narrow strip of land that juts out into the water), the settlers also found it easier to defend themselves against attacks from the Powhatan and Pamunkey Indians. From a military standpoint, the location was ideal.[7]

Jamestown, Virginia, 1607–1610
"Wee Are Fortified Well Against the Indians"

The trip over from England had been long and hard. Almost one third of the group died on the journey from poor nutrition and disease. The remaining 105 settlers and crew who had survived now set about securing their new home by constructing a fort. Completed in June 1607, the fort consisted of a row of stripped logs hewn from nearby trees. These were placed upright and partially buried in a trench, which, as a settler named George Percy noted in his journal, "was trianglewise, having three bulwarks at every corner like a half-moon, and four or five pieces of artillery mounted in them."[8] In a letter sent to the directors of the Virginia Company of London, the corporation that King James I had chartered to settle the southern part of the North American continent, a member of the governing council wrote: "Within lesse than seaven weekes, wee are fortified well against the Indians."[9]

But the colonists also needed someplace to live. As the construction of the fort progressed, the settlers, according to the account written by Captain John Smith, "cut downe trees to make place to pitch . . . Tents," which were humorously referred to by some as "castles in the air." Despite this effort, by the fall of 1607 housing was still inadequate. Smith noted in his journal that there were "no houses to cover us, our Tents were rotten and our Cabbins worse."[10]

The establishment of Jamestown was no easy undertaking, and the colonists often made it more difficult than it would otherwise have been. They committed one serious blunder after another, endangering themselves and the future of the settlement. They were unprepared for the oppressive summer heat, the suffocating humidity, and the sometimes bitter winter cold. Weather conditions were far more extreme in the New World than in England. The settlers also soon learned that the marshes near their new town were infested with mosquitoes, and that as a result they were exposed to malaria, a very serious illness that produced chills and fever, and often death.

Worse, there was no regular source of fresh water. Many colonists suffered from salt poisoning and other diseases after repeatedly drinking the salty, stagnant water of the James River.[11] In the spring, when the English first arrived, the water was safe. Spring rains and high runoff had flushed salt and disease-carrying organisms out to sea; fresh water swirled around Jamestown.[12] The English did not seem to realize, however, that during July and August, when there was little rainfall, the James contained high concentrations of salt from the ocean. It was also contaminated with the bacteria and parasites that cause typhoid and dysentery, which affects the intestines and can be fatal.

Salt poisoning is characterized by swelling of the joints, lack of energy, and irritability. Perhaps some of the lazy and unruly behavior that historians have traditionally associated with the Jamestown colonists can be attributed to this affliction. Colonists also began dying at an alarming rate from typhoid and dysentery; sometimes as many as three or four died in a single day.

In his journal, George Percy observed the outbreak of all three ailments among the colonists. In an entry dated July 9, 1607, Percy recorded the death of George Flowre from "swelling," probably a symptom of salt poisoning. Percy also lamented that "our men were destroyed with cruell diseases, as Swelling [salt poisoning], Flixes [dysentery], Burning Fevers [typhoid] . . . and some departed suddenly."[13]

Illness was not the only problem the settlers faced. The food they had brought from England quickly spoiled; the water became fouled and infested with mosquitoes. Weak from hunger and malnutrition, the colonists could not tend the crops they had planted, which were supposed to feed them through the winter. They did not venture out on hunting and fishing expeditions because they feared the unfriendly Indians who lived nearby, and in any case, they were often too weak and sick to do so.

By the fall, only thirty-eight settlers were still alive. These survivors squabbled bitterly over questions of leadership, raising threats of a mutiny. For the next three years, the colonists struggled just to survive. Only the most foolish continued to entertain thoughts of getting rich.

"In Honor of His Majesty's Name, Jamestown"

Somehow, the colonists did manage to endure the hardships and calamities they faced in the New World. The fort they had built also survived, despite suffering various difficulties of its own. In January 1608, for example, a fire swept through the structure, seriously damaging it. Captain John Smith described the aftermath:

An archaeologist from the Jamestown Rediscovery Team painstakingly brushes away dirt from an excavated leg bone. The movements of archaeologists must be precise so they won't damage the artifact. Courtesy of the Association for the Preservation of Virginia Antiquities.

> James towne being burnt, we rebuilt it . . . invironed with a pal-
> izodo of fourteen or fifteene feet, and each as much as three or
> four men could carrie . . . We had three Bulwarks, four and
> twentie peece of ordinance upon convenient plat-forms.[14]

The fort was quickly rebuilt, with a number of new additions. Now
tucked inside were a storehouse, a church, and between forty and fifty
thatch-roofed houses.[15]

The problems of Jamestown and its inhabitants, though, were just
beginning. The little settlement continued to struggle. Despite the arrival
of new settlers every year, including some women, the town was con-
tinually plagued by illness, food shortages, and uneasy relations with
local Indians. By the spring of 1610, the colony had deteriorated so
severely that the fort was again in shambles, with the "palisades torn
down, the ports open, [and] the gates off their hinges."[16]

Still, the settlers hung on. So did the fort, after some extensive
rebuilding. William Strachey, another of the Jamestown settlers, provided
the most complete description of the structure:

> the fort . . . about half an acre . . . is cast almost in the form of a
> triangle and so pallisaded. The south side next the river . . . con-
> tains 140 yards, the west and east sides a hundred only. At every
> angle or corner, where the lines meet, a bulwark or watchtower is
> raised and in each bulwark a piece or two well mounted. . . . And
> thus enclosed, as I said, round with a palisade of planks and
> strong posts, four feet deep in the ground, of young oaks, wal-
> nuts, etc. . . the fort is called, in honor of his majesty's name,
> Jamestown. The principal gate from the town, through the
> palisade, opens to the river, as at each bulwark there is a gate
> likewise.[17]

Eventually the colonists abandoned the triangular wooden structure
that Strachey described and, in 1639, built a new brick fort.

Although it became the first capital of the Virginia colony, Jamestown continued its slow but steady decline. In 1698, nearly sixty years after the colonists had rebuilt the fort, the statehouse was destroyed in a fire. That same year, colonial officials decided to move the capital from Jamestown to Williamsburg. By that time, it seemed as if the life of the Jamestown settlement had already departed. Although the town continued to operate as a ferry crossing, many of the residents moved away. Some relocated to the thriving towns of Williamsburg and Yorktown, while others moved westward along the James River as the Indians retreated. Jamestown quietly disappeared, at least above the ground. The only visible reminder of the settlement's existence was the dilapidated church tower.

Jamestown Island, April 1994
We Knew We Had Found It!

In April 1994, Kelso returned to Jamestown Island to dig. By then he was an accomplished and respected archaeologist, and the director of archaeology for the Association for the Preservation of Virginia Antiquities, or APVA. The organization was beginning to plan for the quadricentennial, or 400-year anniversary of the founding of Jamestown, scheduled to take place in 2007. To commemorate such a momentous occasion, the organization needed a very special project. Kelso had an idea: why not search for the original Jamestown fort? The APVA's first response? "They thought I was crazy," Kelso recalled.[18]

Yet Kelso convinced the directors of the APVA to allow him to give his proposal a try. To skeptics who charged that the fort had disappeared, Kelso offered his argument, carefully thought out during the past thirty years:

> Until now, no one had doubted that the settlers were a bunch
> of lazy people who weren't doing anything, so they starved.
> They were called "gentleman," but no one realized that gentle-

men could be seasoned soldiers. They had enough military sense not to build the fort in a place that would erode away.[19]

Armed with that conviction, Kelso looked to the island for answers.

By now, a number of excavations had been done at the Jamestown site. The first efforts began in 1889, when the APVA acquired the 22 1/2 acres where the traditional Jamestown site had once existed. That same year, an extensive ten-year excavation project to preserve the church tower began. In 1930, the National Park Service established the Colonial National Historical Park, which placed the remaining 1500 acres of the island under government protection. For the next twelve years, additional archaeological work was conducted. Concentrating on five acres in the area of the old church, archaeologists uncovered a variety of early seventeenth-century artifacts as well as remains dating from the later colonial period. But while the archaeologists believed that the fort had in fact been located in this general area, they also concluded that the fort had washed away.

Based on the earlier excavation work, Kelso theorized that the fort was located in one of three areas. The first was the place at which the ground appeared to sag into a hole that had been excavated and then refilled with dirt. The second was near one of the modern service roads. The third was in a covered, shady area.[20] Kelso pinpointed these three spots because each was in the vicinity of the Jamestown fort's church. Although Kelso knew that the church had been rebuilt at least five times, he also thought that in all probability the location of the church had not changed since 1607. He thus determined to begin excavations in the three areas that stood between the church and the seawall. If remains of the fort had survived, he expected to find them in one of those three sites.

Near the place where Kelso had stood thirty years before, doubting the accepted explanations of the fort's disappearance, was "a piece of ground, shaped like a triangle that no one had ever put a shovel into. By the time I put that shovel into the ground," Kelso recollected, "very smart people had convinced me that I was wrong. But I wanted to try. I would have felt much worse if I hadn't."[21]

Kelso and his Jamestown Rediscovery Team got to work at once. Before long, they discovered bits of broken pottery mixed with the dirt, mud, clay, and shale. In his excitement, Kelso could hardly believe his eyes. The tiny shards could only have come from one place. After more than thirty years of wondering, doubting, and hoping, Kelso had found the original Jamestown fort![22]

During the next two years, the site, overlooked for nearly 400 years, willingly yielded its treasures. Kelso and his team even uncovered impressions left in the earth by the fort's rotting wooden posts and corner watchtowers. By using their mathematical skills and a tiny drawing made in 1608, the team sketched an outline of the fort. Much to their relief, they realized that the James River had claimed only one corner of the structure. Most of the fort, almost 80 percent of the original structure, was on dry land.[23]

An aerial view of the Jamestown Rediscovery excavation area, September 1996, with a superimposed digital reconstruction of the palisade that surrounded the settlement.
Courtesy of the Association for the Preservation of Virginia Antiquities.

For the next two-and-a-half years, Kelso and his crew of six special-
ists unearthed a list of artifacts that reads like a catalog of seventeenth-
century colonial life: small toys, copper and glass beads, keys, pottery,
pipes, medical instruments, Dutch and English coins, armor, and fragments of weaponry. To their astonishment, they even found a signet ring
decorated with a bird crest that had belonged to William Strachey, whose
description of the fort was invaluable to Kelso during his investigation.
By November 1996, after recovering more than 180,000 artifacts, Kelso
and his crew had to stop digging; they had run out of storage space. Yet
only 5 percent of the site had been excavated![24]

The biggest surprise was yet to come. On a rainy September day in
1996, Kelso and his colleagues were busy at the site when they stumbled
onto something quite unexpected. Lying in a rotting wooden coffin,
covered with 400 years of dirt and mud, was a skeleton. The Jamestown
Rediscovery Team had just met one of the fort's original inhabitants.

Jamestown Fort, August 15, 1607
Murder!

The mood at the fort was tense. Many of the Jamestown colonists were
already sick or dying, and there was little respite from the oppressive heat
that added to their suffering. To make matters worse, the daily rations
consisted of little more than wormy wheat and stale barley. The threat
from Indian attack was ever-present. Then there were the strained relations among the settlers themselves.

For months, the colonists had been quarreling over the leadership
of the settlement. They divided basically into two groups: those who
supported the current leadership of Edward Maria Wingfield, who had
been appointed president of the settlement by the Virginia Company,
and those who favored Captain John Smith. Wingfield's supporters grew
increasingly uneasy at the possibility that there would be a mutiny and
Smith would seize power. If tensions continued to mount, many of
Wingfield's followers feared they might have to resort to violence to

quell an uprising before it got started.

During the early morning hours of August 15, 1607, someone murdered a young gentleman soldier who was standing guard in one of the watchtowers above the Jamestown fort. The assailant had fired from below, and the shot destroyed most of his unfortunate victim's lower leg. The shell probably severed the femoral artery just below the knee, and in minutes the wounded man bled to death. Less than twenty-four hours later, the victim was placed in a wooden coffin and given a Christian burial not more than 100 yards from the southeast bulwark where he had died. Records contain no other information about the identity of the victim or the way in which he died. For 389 years, no one gave another thought to the unsolved murder.

Jamestown Fort, September 12, 1996
Meet JR102C

It took fourteen hours for the members of Kelso's archaeological team to remove the coffin and its inhabitant. They did so by bracing a half-ton of the surrounding dirt, clay, and mud with special straps and pieces of metal and wood. The team then moved their find to a protective tent. After cleaning away the dirt, they immediately established a few facts. The skeleton was that of a young male, about five feet, five inches tall. Based on the development of the skeleton's wisdom teeth, Kelso and his team guessed that he was between the ages of nineteen and twenty-two at the time of his death. The remains of the coffin and the shroud pin suggested he had been a man of some wealth. Based on the type of dirt and the artifacts found in the coffin, the team concluded that the skeleton was among the fort's first inhabitants, perhaps even one of the "54 gentlemen" listed in Captain John Smith's register.[25]

It was on closer inspection that Kelso discovered evidence of a large gunshot wound near the right calf, almost certainly made by a .60-caliber lead ball. The ball eventually came to rest just beneath the skeleton's kneecap. The skeleton presented some new and startling data about life

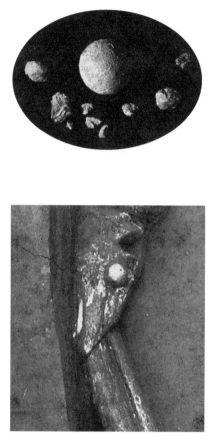

(Right) The skeleton of JR102C, soon to be known as "J.R."

(Top left) The team matched fragments of the lead shot found in J.R.'s knee with those of an identical ball of lead to determine what kind of ammunition killed him.

(Bottom left) A closeup of J.R.'s leg detailing the fatal bullet wound just below the right knee. Courtesy of the Association for the Preservation of Virginia Antiquities.

in Jamestown. Kelso and his team knew, of course, that death had come to Jamestown in many forms: starvation, Indian attacks, and disease. But suddenly they had to confront an unforeseen and unsettling reality: death by murder.[26] The angle and range of the shot suggested that someone had stood no more than three feet from the victim and fired upward. Although other theories such as a possible Indian attack or even an accidental discharge from the victim's own gun were discussed, it was soon clear that something more sinister had taken place. From the outset Kelso sensed "that shot . . . was intended to kill."[27]

Soon after it was discovered, the skeleton, which the team nicknamed "J. R." for Jamestown Rediscovery, was on its way to the on-site laboratory for further study and testing. Aided by forensic experts, Kelso hoped to determine the skeleton's identity and possibly explain the time and circumstances of his death.

By 1997, the team thought they knew their man. Stephen Calthrop, the third son of a wealthy landowner in Norwich, England, had come to Virginia to seek his fortune, since he was unlikely to inherit much of his father's property. Calthrop would have been of the right age and background. There was a record of his death on August 15, 1607, but no cause was listed. He had allied himself with Captain John Smith, and may have helped Smith in plotting a mutiny against the Wingfield faction. No wonder, then, that those who kept the records of the colony, probably connected with Wingfield, failed to report the cause of Calthrop's death. Had they done so, they would have been exposing the guilt of one of their confederates, Calthrop's murderer. Calthrop fit the physical evidence based on the information gathered by the Jamestown Rediscovery Team, and his murder made sense historically. But Kelso and his colleagues still were not entirely sure that J.R.'s remains were those of Stephen Calthrop.[28]

Whoever he was, J.R. was not alone for long. A year later, the team found another burial site, three feet north of the first grave. The skeleton it contained was that of a woman, four feet, eight inches tall, and approximately thirty-five years old. She may have been one of two women who survived the settlement's early years. Like J. R./Calthrop, "First Lady" showed evidence of the hard life in seventeenth-century Jamestown. At the time of her death, she had only five teeth left. Experts speculated that she had lost most of them long before her death, since her gums had completely closed over the tooth sockets.[29]

Kelso and the team wondered who First Lady was and how she had died. But they were more interested in how she and the other colonists lived. Were they as lazy and quarrelsome as historians have made them out to be? Did the many different types of weapons and ammunition discovered at the site of the Jamestown fort speak of a time that was violent and dangerous? What did the various pieces of copper, glass beads, and other artifacts that have been unearthed reveal about life in seventeenth-century Virginia?

These questions and others have come to preoccupy the Jamestown Rediscovery Team. Slowly, the answers are coming. As Bill Kelso sees it, "We don't dig things up, we uncover them. You just can't hurry it up."[30]

Kelso and the Jamestown Rediscovery Team have come to some tentative conclusions based on their findings. The glass beads and bits of copper, they think, point to trade activity with the Indians. Other pieces of glass found at the site point to a small industry at Jamestown: glassmaking. No doubt some of the first Jamestown craftsmen had hoped that their skills would be used to make articles out of more precious metals such as gold or silver. Instead of working with the valuable metals, however, they experimented with glass.

The vast array of artifacts also suggests that the English used Jamestown as a dumping ground for outdated armor, weapons, artillery, and other merchandise. The colonies of all imperial powers, not merely those of England, routinely provided ready markets for surplus or unwanted goods that merchants could not sell elsewhere. This arrangement obviously benefitted the economy of the mother country, but it also ensured that the colonies would receive a steady influx of goods, such as

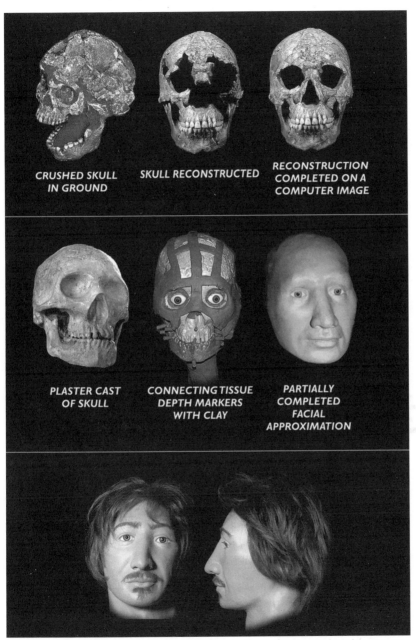

CRUSHED SKULL
IN GROUND

SKULL RECONSTRUCTED

RECONSTRUCTION
COMPLETED ON A
COMPUTER IMAGE

PLASTER CAST
OF SKULL

CONNECTING TISSUE
DEPTH MARKERS
WITH CLAY

PARTIALLY
COMPLETED
FACIAL
APPROXIMATION

Despite serious damage to J.R.'s skull, scientific expertise and computer imaging are combined with an artist's skill to create a picture of what the young man might have looked like. Courtesy of the Association for the Preservation of Virginia Antiquities.

arms and tools, although not necessarily the most fashionable or reliable products.[31]

Kelso estimates that work on the Jamestown site will continue for at least another ten years. He hopes the answers to the many questions the site raises will keep coming; he knows the questions will. Kelso has reason to be optimistic. Since Jamestown did not grow like other colonial settlements and it was eventually abandoned and permitted to fall into ruin, the wealth of artifacts dating from the time of original settlement has been relatively undisturbed by the normal processes of demolition and rebuilding. Even the excavations that took place late in the nineteenth century, after the APVA acquired the property, did not disturb many of the artifacts.[32] Nor did the work done during the 1940s and 1950s under the auspices of the National Park Service, which managed the site in conjunction with the APVA beginning in 1930.[33]

Jamestown, Kelso declares, is an "archaeological time capsule, free from the destructive forces of industrial age construction."[34] He might have added that experts have also recognized the Jamestown Rediscovery Project as "the premier [archeological] find in the United States in this century."[35]

II.

The Search for La Salle:
The Raising of *La Belle*

"I feel as though I'm reaching across 300 years to shake his hand."
—J. Barto Arnold III, marine archaeologist, 1997

Beautiful, yet treacherous, Matagorda Bay is known as the "grave-yard of the Texas Gulf." The bay itself is a broad, sheltered body of water, accessible only by a narrow passage that helmsmen once had to navigate with care. At its deepest point the bay is only eighteen feet, and the sand bars and shifting shoals concealed beneath the surface of the water made navigation even more difficult. The bay was once the primary seaport of the Texas Gulf, and it has welcomed somewhere between 200 and 300 sunken ships to its murky depths. It made no difference under which flags they sailed, whether French, Spanish, or American; all came to rest in the same watery grave. Subject to sudden storms and unpredictable winds, the bay often brought a long journey to a disastrous conclusion.

In 1995, Matagorda Bay reluctantly surrendered one of its most famous treasures: a small frigate christened *La Belle*, which, more than three centuries before, had been part of a French expeditionary fleet. As archaeologists studied the remains of *La Belle* and the artifacts that had survived with her, they began to bring into clearer focus the daring men who accompanied her on her journey to the New World and their king's bold dream to create a vast North American empire.

Roucheford, France, 1684
Commanded by "Two Masters"

Her name was *La Belle*, meaning "The Beautiful," and she was no ordinary vessel. Commissioned by King Louis XIV of France and designed by the master shipwright Pierre Mallet, *La Belle* was constructed in 1684 at the shipyards in the city of Roucheford. The king gave the ship as a gift to the French explorer Sieur de La Salle.

La Belle was not large by the standards of the day. When finished, she measured fifty-one feet in length from bow to stern (front to back), fourteen feet in width, and probably weighed between forty and forty-five tons, though contemporary accounts place the ship's weight closer to sixty. Categorized as a *barque longue,* or a "long ship," *La Belle* was actually the smallest type of ocean-going frigate to sail the seas during the late seventeenth century. *La Belle* boasted two masts with square sails and could defend herself with the help of six cannon. Additional firepower came from a number of swivel guns mounted on the railing. Her operation required a crew of between twenty and thirty men.[1] But a mere description of *La Belle* does not reveal her real significance. As Henri Joutel, a member of La Salle's expedition who would chronicle the journey in his diary, noted, the vessel served "two masters": La Salle and King Louis himself.[2]

In making a gift of *La Belle* to La Salle, Louis XIV entertained dreams of creating an empire. Four years earlier, in 1680, the fearless La Salle had led the first group of Frenchmen down the Mississippi River, a treacherous journey that began on the Illinois River and ended at the mouth of the Mississippi in the Gulf of Mexico. On April 9, 1682, La Salle had claimed for France the vast interior of the North American continent. He called the land "Louisiana" in honor of his king.[3] Now Louis wanted La Salle, along with approximately 300 French soldiers, sailors, and colonists, to return to the New World and assert French claims to additional territory in North America.[4] By extending French authority in America, Louis hoped, at the same time, to strike a blow against the ambitions of the hated Spanish.

While the Spanish had been building their overseas empire in the Caribbean, Mexico, and South America during the first decades of the sixteenth century, the French had also been developing an interest in the New World. In 1534, Jacques Cartier explored the St. Lawrence River as far as present-day Montreal. He established the colony of Charlesbourg-Royal near the site of modern Quebec in 1541, but the colony failed when the French settlers withdrew to escape the harsh winters. In 1562, nearly thirty years after Cartier had made the first extended forays into eastern Canada, another French explorer, Jean Ribault, headed an expedition to the St. Johns River in Florida. A second French mission under the leadership of René de Laudonnierè investigated the same region in 1564. The Spanish, however, soon drove the French out of Florida. From then on, the French concentrated their attention and their efforts on the northern and western regions of North America.

In 1608, Samuel de Champlain built a fort on the present site of Quebec and explored the area north of Port Royal, Nova Scotia. Champlain traveled as far south as Cape Cod, located in what is today southeastern Massachusetts. By 1672, New France, as the French empire in North America was known, had a population of more than 5,000 inhabitants. In 1673, Father Jacques Marquette and Louis Joliet located the Mississippi River, which nine years later La Salle would travel all the way to the Gulf of Mexico. Now, enjoying the full confidence and support of the king, La Salle prepared to set out again with the intention of establishing a French colony in the Louisiana Territory.

"On the 24th of July, 1684," reported Henri Joutel, "the Sieur de La Salle . . . departed. We had four ships [including] a small frigate called the *Belle* of about 60 tons armed with six cannon."[5] *La Belle* was accompanied by the *Joly*, a man-of-war armed with thirty-six cannon, the *Aimable*, a large, 300-ton transport vessel that carried most of the provisions for the settlement, and the thirty-ton *Saint François*, a smaller two-masted vessel, that would convey perishables such as wine, meat, and vegetables as far as the French colony of Saint Domingue (now Haiti). There the expedition planned to take on fresh water, additional supplies, and a party of thirty buccaneers to reinforce the troops who had traveled from France with La Salle.

In their four sturdy vessels, the explorers were to cross the Atlantic and land at the mouth of the Mississippi River. Three hundred persons set out with La Salle on the journey. Settlers and tradesmen, including carpenters, toolmakers, and masons, along with a handful of clergymen, among them La Salle's older brother, and 100 soldiers were part of the expedition. Four women, two of whom were married, and at least six children, were also onboard.

Once they landed at the Mississippi, La Salle was to lead his group approximately 180 miles upriver where they would build a fort. Along the way, La Salle hoped to recruit some 15,000 Native American allies to help the French conduct raids on Spanish forts and eventually to seize the rich Spanish silver mines in northern Mexico. What made the entire venture unusually dangerous was that a century earlier Philip II, then the king of Spain, had declared the entire region surrounding the Gulf of Mexico off-limits to all foreigners under pain of death. In effect, La Salle and his party were attempting to establish a French colony in territory that the Spanish had long regarded their own.[6] If the Spanish discovered La Salle's band of soldiers and settlers, they would almost certainly execute them on the spot.

Matagorda Bay, Texas Coast, 1995
"That Personal Connection with the Past"

The archaeologists knew it was out there, somewhere beneath the waters of the bay. Since 1978, under the direction of the Texas Historical Commission, a team of archaeologists, divers, and researchers had studied Matagorda Bay in the hope of finding La Salle's lost ship. Headed by marine archaeologist J. Barto Arnold III, the team had been patiently charting underwater anomalies, searching the depths for anything unusual or out of place. They detected such anomalies with the help of sophisticated electronic surveillance equipment designed especially for underwater use. One of the most important devices they employed was the magnetometer sensor, which they towed behind their ship. The magnetometer sensor alerted the team to the presence of metal in the water. It transmitted the data directly to the ship's computer for the archaeologists to catalog and interpret.

The problem with the magnetometer sensor was that it did not distinguish between the types of metal detected. For all the crew knew, they could be reading the location of a rusty iron anchor, a coil of wire, or even what they called a "ghost," traces of metal that remained in the water long after the object that produced them had deteriorated. To help them pinpoint the location of *La Belle*, the archaeologists also relied on maps, histories, and any other sources—including the testimony of local fishermen—that could provide clues about where the ship had gone down. Some of the most promising documents, ironically, were seventeenth-century Spanish accounts that described the wreckage of the ship and gave its approximate location.

For Arnold, the quest to locate La Salle's ship was not just a job, it was a lifelong ambition. Although originally trained as a land archaeologist, Arnold made the jump "from shore to sea" after he took a job cleaning artifacts recovered from two Spanish galleons. The work so fascinated him that he changed the direction of his career. Now, as chief marine archaeologist for the state of Texas, Arnold was intent on finding La Salle's lost ship. Not only would it be the end of a seventeen-year search, but to Arnold, it would be an exciting way to "make that personal connection with the past."[7]

Matagorda Bay, Spanish North America, January 1685-1688
"A Large and Vast Country"

From the outset, La Salle's expedition was in trouble. No sooner had his ships departed France then they encountered a terrible storm. The *Joly* was so badly damaged that it could not continue the voyage. Under the circumstances, La Salle decided that all four vessels had to return to port until workmen completed the necessary repairs. At last, on August 1, 1684, the ships set sail once more.

After only three months at sea, the *Saint François* fell into the hands of Spanish pirates near the island of Hispaniola, the present site of Haiti and the Dominican Republic. (At various times, the French and the Spanish had controlled this island, and eventually they divided it. The French called their colony Saint Domingue, which is now Haiti, and the Spanish called theirs Hispaniola or, alternately, Santo Domingo, which is now the Dominican Republic). After restocking the three remaining ships, La Salle sailed for the Gulf of Mexico. By December 28, 1684, lookouts had sighted land. But La Salle, unfamiliar with the Louisiana coastline, had relied on inaccurate maps. Lacking the technology to determine longitude, and having made a two-degree error in calculating latitude because of a faulty astrolabe, he missed the mouth of the Mississippi River and sailed some 400 miles west of his original destination.[8]

On February 18, 1685, La Salle's ships laid anchor in Matagorda Bay, an inlet off the Gulf of Mexico between what are today the cities of Corpus Christi and Galveston, Texas. The American historian Francis Parkman described the scene in a book published 200 years later: "The aspect of the country was not cheering, with its barren plains, its reedy marshes, its interminable oyster beds, and broad flats of mud bare at low tide."[9]

Greater misfortunes awaited. An outbreak of scurvy ravaged La Salle's men. They suffered the usual symptoms of spongy gums, loosening teeth, and bleeding under the skin caused by a deficiency of ascorbic acid in their diets. Rattlesnakes and alligators also plagued the French. A rattlesnake bit Sieur Le Gros, one of La Salle's best and most reliable men. Although his leg was amputated, Le Gros died anyway. Several other of La Salle's men, along with a number of colonists, died from eating poisonous berries. Still another problem distressed La Salle. None of the eight native languages he spoke enabled him to communicate with the Karankawa Indians, who were unfriendly and menacing. The Karankawa, in fact, killed several men who had decided to spend a night on shore, and took a number of others captive.

It was in February 1685, while La Salle was away negotiating with the Karankawa for the release of the prisoners, that the *Aimable* ran aground on a sand bar, a high ridge of sand below the surface of the water. The damage she sustained was too extensive to repair and the ship sank. The explorers managed to salvage gunpowder, wine, food, and timbers with which to build their fort, but many other irreplaceable supplies sank to the bottom. The next month, Taneguy le Gallois de Beaujeu, captain of the *Joly*, concluded that he had fulfilled his obligations to the expedition. He abandoned La Salle and sailed for France. Beaujeu had never liked La Salle. Since the beginning of the journey, Beaujeu, an officer in the French navy, had resented taking orders from a man who, he said, "has no experience of war except with savages, . . . who has no rank, and never commanded anybody but school boys."[10]

Despite Beaujeu's departure and the other setbacks and hardships the French endured, La Salle did not give up his dream of finding the mouth of the Mississippi River. In March, accompanied by fifty-two of his men, he left on a scouting mission to locate a site on which to establish a permanent settlement. By April, he had selected a location and construction of the first buildings began.

At the chosen place, La Salle's men set about building a crude fort using wood cut from the trees they cleared and the planks salvaged from the ruined *Aimable*. Within the confines of the fort, they also built another structure that consisted of four rooms: one for La Salle, another for one of the priests who had accompanied the expedition, a third to house several of the men, and the fourth to serve as a storehouse. Because the weather was still mild, many of the settlers slept comfortably outside. Still others built crude wooden shelters for themselves.

Eventually, the French built another structure of two rooms: one for the women and another for the men. They covered this wooden dormitory with reeds and topped it with a clay-and-plank roof. To this primitive community the French gave the name Fort St. Louis.

"Stranded"

By January 1686, the situation had become grim. La Salle had lost more than half of his men to desertion, disease, and death. The livestock that the French had brought from France had long since died, and their agricultural efforts had failed. The fruits and vegetables grown so easily in French soil proved no match for the hot, humid, and salty air of the gulf. La Salle's small but distinguished fleet now numbered only one ship: *La Belle*. Worse, La Salle finally admitted that he was lost in what Henri Joutel described in his journal as "a large and vast country."[11] Morale was low and tensions were high between La Salle and his men.[12]

The situation, in fact, could not have been more grave. Food supplies were dwindling. Disease was rampant. Relations with the Karankawa were still dangerously strained. Endless battles with mosquitoes, snakes, and alligators left the settlers sick, exhausted, frightened, and desperate. As if circumstances were not bad enough, La Salle had gone off on a scouting mission in search of the elusive Mississippi River. *La Belle* was not close at hand; it was anchored near Lavaca Bay, not far from the spot from which La Salle had departed. He had promised to return in a few days, but it was, instead, three months before he, and what remained of his scouting party, made their way back to the fort. By then, the unthinkable had happened.

Shortly after La Salle had left in January 1686, the men aboard *La Belle* had run out of drinking water; several sailors perished from dehydration. In the midst of the crisis, Monsieur Teissier, the master of the vessel, panicked and began drinking brandy. He even consumed the sacramental wine that was to be used during the celebration of Mass. When five desperate sailors took the only skiff onboard and headed for shore in search of fresh water, Teissier, who by this time was very drunk, set out a single candle instead of a lantern to guide them back to the ship in the darkness. The candle quickly burned out, and the men who tried to get ashore disappeared, never to be seen again.[13]

In February 1686, remaining crew members, although weak, sick, and near despair, sailed for Fort St. Louis. Unfortunately, they were too unskilled and too undermanned to handle the ship. To make a bad situation even worse, before the French could reach the fort a "blue norther," one of the severe storms that periodically blows down from the north, thundered through the bay. *La Belle* was no match for the near hurricane-force winds. Dragging the anchor did not steady the ship; the sailors could not stop her from listing to one side. At last, *La Belle*, out of control, ran aground on one of the many underwater sand bars that riddled the bay.[14] Sieur Chefdeville, one of the two priests who had come over with the expedition related that all onboard were drowned, except for six, who had miraculously found a canoe and made their way to the fort. In mid-March, when La Salle and his group returned to the site and found the ship gone, they had no choice but to walk back to the fort. By late March, they had returned, but still did not know what had happened to *La Belle*.

Two months passed. Then one day, Henri Joutel recorded in his journal:

> At about two o'clock on the afternoon on May 1, as I was walking around the house, I heard from the lower stretch of the river a voice that cried out several times, "Who goes there?". . . . Again I heard the same voice. . . . But when I came near the riverbank I heard voices which I was not accustomed to hearing.[15]

The voice Joutel recognized among the rest was that of Sieur Chefdeville. Worried that something was terribly wrong, Joutel hurried to the bank, asking what had become of the *Belle*. From the priest, who had been onboard the vessel, Joutel learned the particulars of the disaster that had occurred in February. Joutel later recounted Chefdeville's story in his diary:

> she had perished, or rather gone aground. . . and. . . . only six
> had escaped. . . . I took them up to the house and had unloaded
> from their canoe a number of things, among others, La Salle's
> clothes and some of his papers, some linen and glass beads, and
> 30 to 40 pounds of meal. . . . We were distressed by the loss of
> the ship.[16]

The settlers had every reason to lament this disturbing turn of events,
for it left them even more alone, stranded, and vulnerable than before.

Claimed by the Sea

La Belle remained mired on the sand bar. A little more than a year later,
in April 1687, Spanish explorers found her still resting there. Though
her deck was awash, they managed to rescue several cannon and a part
of the rigging. The bay, though, slowly claimed *La Belle* as its own. A
year and half after the initial Spanish call, another Spanish expedition
came upon the ship. All that remained by this time was a pile of rotting,
bolt-studded boards, a few rusty wrenches, and some cases of broken
muskets. Gradually the hull settled into the thick covering of sand and
silt that protected it from the elements for the next 300 years.[17]

La Salle's dream of founding a French empire in the New World suffered a similarly dismal fate. It died with him on March 20, 1687, when
his own men ambushed and murdered him. At the time of his death,
La Salle may have been wearing the canvas clothing fashioned from
La Belle's sails, the last gift of the vessel to her master. The twenty or so
settlers who remained at Fort St. Louis fared no better. Sometime in
late December 1687 or early January 1688, Karankawa Indians, learning
that La Salle had been missing for some time (he was already dead, but
the Indians did not know it), attacked the settlement, killing the adults
and all except five of the children, whom they carried off. Traveling with
the remnants of La Salle's scouting party, Henri Joutel eventually made

his way to a small French outpost along the Illinois River. From there he returned to Montreal and then to France. Joutel was one of fewer than a dozen survivors out of the roughly 300 persons who had left France three years earlier as part of La Salle's grand enterprise.

Like *La Belle*, Fort St. Louis also gradually disappeared. The second Spanish expedition that had earlier come upon the remains of the ship later found what was left of the French settlement. It had been reduced to little more than rotting, tumble-down cabins, with the doors torn from their hinges. Traces of household goods were strewn on the ground, ruined by long exposure to the elements. Scattered among the debris were the remains of the settlers themselves, one woman still gripping a shirt in her hand.[18] In due course, the Spaniards observed, time and nature would consume these last vestiges as well.

Matagorda Bay, Texas, July 1995
Site #41MG86

It had been a busy month. Aboard their research vessel, the *Anomaly*, the crew had spent most of their time surveying and mapping the various underwater anomalies that the magnetometer sensor had detected. Finally, after years of searching, Arnold and his colleagues sensed that they were closing in on the location of *La Belle*. Now all they needed was something every archaeologist hopes for: a stroke of good luck.

One hot July morning it appeared that the final piece of the puzzle had at last fallen into place. The team was at work in a section of the bay near Port O'Connor, where divers had located what seemed to be the remains of a ship's hull in about twelve feet of water. The ship was in the general area where Arnold and his team believed *La Belle* had gone down. Soon team members were examining artifacts that the magnetometer sensor had detected and that divers had retrieved. They included musket balls, small bronze bells, and an old belt buckle. Clearly, the items were of another era. But were they from *La Belle*?

The dark, murky waters of Matagorda Bay made it difficult for the divers to see underwater, even with the benefit of artificial lighting. As a consequence, they had to rely more on touch than on sight. On the second dive of the day, Chuck Meide thought he felt something unusual. As he explored further, it appeared that he had found a raised handle of the sort used to lift a cannon. Meide recalled, "If it was a cannon, I knew exactly where the other handle ought to be." He reached out his hand and there it was. "My diving partner claims she could hear me screaming underwater," he laughed.[19]

Meide, though, was still unsure. Running his hands along the object, he felt both its shape and its length. There could be no question. Although heavily encrusted with centuries of calcium deposits, it was the clue that Chuck Meide and his associates had all been looking for: a cannon dating back to the seventeenth century! Meide returned to the surface as quickly as possible to break the news to the team. Arnold was elated. After three centuries, Matagorda Bay had finally given up *La Belle*.[20]

A cannon from La Belle *found by diver Chuck Meide. One of the two arching dolphin handles is at the top of the cannon.* Photo courtesy of Texas Historical Commission.

Raising the *Belle*

A few days after their discovery, the team members carefully tied ropes around the 793-pound cannon and, with the help of a crane, hauled it to the surface. After gently cleaning away the calcium deposits that had built up on the piece, the team found that the handles Chuck Meide had so eagerly grasped were the sculpted forms of two arching dolphins, a characteristic of ship's cannon manufactured during the seventeenth century. The team also found a sculpted "*L*" topped with a crown to represent King Louis XIV. There could be no doubt now what they had found.[21]

Arnold felt sure *La Belle* was "one of the most important shipwrecks that's ever been dug in this continent." Now he faced the challenge of how best to recover it. In similar cases, divers had performed underwater excavations, examining artifacts and noting their locations. In the murky waters of Matagorda Bay, however, such a procedure was unworkable. To complicate matters, *La Belle* had come to rest in an anaerobic environment, that is, in an environment without oxygen. The moment the hull was exposed to the oxygen in the air, it would begin to deteriorate. Arnold, therefore, had to find a way to study the hull and its contents without endangering them.

It was at this point that someone at the Texas Historical Commission suggested a daring method of exploring *La Belle*. Instead of bringing the wreckage to the surface, he proposed the construction of a cofferdam, a double-walled watertight structure that would allow archaeologists to work on the site as if it were dry land, even though it remained under twelve feet of water! The cofferdam would be built around the site and the seawater pumped out, exposing the ship, which would still be covered by its protective coating of mud and silt.[22]

Marine archeologists had used cofferdams in Europe to excavate underwater sites. In the United States, though, they were still relatively untried. Only once had such a device been used, to excavate a sunken Civil War vessel in the James River during the late 1970s. What the Texas Historical Commission proposed was very new.

In the summer of 1996, construction of the cofferdam began. The structure consisted of two concentric octagonal walls made of $3/8$-foot-thick steel plates called "sheet pilings" that surrounded the submerged hull. The outer wall measured 148 feet long by 118 feet wide, the inner wall was 82 feet by 52 feet. Assembled in pairs, the walls rested on sheet pilings that had been inserted to a depth of forty-one feet below the floor of the bay. The outer wall of the cofferdam extended approximately six-and-a-half feet above the surface of the water and held the water back. Large bucket loads of sand were emptied between the two walls. A mobile crane, operating on a specially constructed track that ran on the sand between the inner and outer walls, lifted the artifacts found in the ship's hull out of the water and placed them onto a transport barge. The barge, which was docked at the site, would bring the

The cofferdam, showing the sand-filled walls and the transport barges in the foreground. The ship's hull is under the steel roof and the crane, used to hoist the findings, lies braced on the sand (rear, left). Photo courtesy of Texas Historical Commission.

artifacts to the conservation laboratory located on the campus of Texas A & M University. A steel roof shielded the inner portion of the site, where the hull lay, from the elements, while an observation deck enabled onlookers to watch the work in progress.[23] With the cofferdam in place, Arnold thought the chances were excellent for a successful excavation of *La Belle*.[24]

"A Most Romantic Find"

In the late summer of 1996, the archaeology team set to work. Operating from special metal runners that served as working platforms allowed the team to move about but never to tread upon the site itself. The archaeologists hoped that none of the fragile artifacts would be lost. Carefully using their trowels, they placed mud from the site into buckets. The buckets were then hoisted by the crane to the deck of the support barge where the team members carefully looked for any artifacts from the ship that might be hidden in the mud.

In time, the outline of *La Belle*'s hull began to emerge, and with it the goods that the French had packed into the ship's hold. Team members took the measurement of each artifact they found, and plotted its location on a graph. They then placed the artifacts on metal screens with openings so small that nothing but silt would fall through and removed them to a special screening area where the objects were washed with high-pressure hoses. Then each object was numbered. If the archaeologists ever managed to resurrect or recreate the hull on land, they would be able to replace each one of the items exactly where it belonged. They hoped that in time each plank of the hull would also be carefully dismantled for transport to the conservation lab. These procedures were slow and tedious, but for Arnold and the team the effort was worth it. He explained that "every nail, every fastening, every board, every piece of rigging will tell us a story that's not known."[25]

During the next eight months, the archaeologists worked seven days a week to uncover the secrets of *La Belle*. To their surprise and delight, they learned that the ship had been carefully packed by La

Salle's crew in three sections. As team members moved from section to section, they were amazed at the wealth of artifacts preserved in the hull. Starting at the bow, the archaeologists discovered an assortment of supplies, including a 600-foot coil of anchor rope. Upon closer inspection, the team found something else curled inside the rope: a human skeleton! Next to the remains were a leather pouch, a pair of shoes, and some buttons. The skeleton was so well preserved that the team even discovered traces of the brain inside the skull. The archaeologists suspected that the skeleton belonged to one of the sailors who had either died from dehydration or who drowned when the ship ran aground. Subsequent examinations revealed that the sailor was about forty-five years old at the time of his death and that he suffered from arthritis.[26]

Moving on to the midsection of the ship, the team uncovered a genuine treasure trove, with items packed "right where the French put them before the wreck."[27] Lying in the storage compartments of the hold were a dazzling array of practical items that the colonists no doubt intended to use in setting up and running their households. These included brass

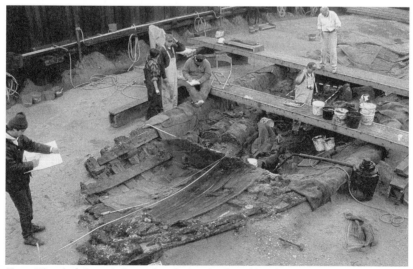

Texas Historical Commission archaeologists sketch and log the items uncovered in the storage compartment located in the midsection of the ship. Note the two intact wooden casks that were found here. Photo courtesy of Texas Historical Commission.

pots for cooking, pewter plates for eating, pottery of various kinds, wooden casks with willow hoop handles still intact, probably used for storing wine or water; candlesticks, straight pins, and wooden combs with teeth on both sides. The team speculated that these were for combing hair on one side and combing out lice on the other. They also uncovered a variety of tools, such as roping, rigging, and axe heads. In addition, divers brought to the surface wooden beads and a small gilded cross, possibly the remains of a rosary; a ruby ring; and nine leather shoes.[28] Finally, the archaeologists discovered weapons and ammunition of every description, such as swivel guns, an ample supply of lead shot, cannonballs, and muskets with their stocks still recognizable.

Goods presumably meant for trading with the Indians included a box containing almost one million tiny glass beads in blue, white, and black that the Indians might have used for decoration and beadwork. There were several small pieces of glass that could have been used as mirrors, some of which the French probably also proposed to barter in transactions with the Indians. The archaeologists found several dozen small bronze bells of the kind used in the sport of falconry. It is unlikely that the French colonists in the New World were going to train falcons for hunting, but possibly they hoped also to trade the bells to the Indians. Among the jewelry found were so-called Jesuit rings, tiny brass rings engraved with religious designs. These provided evidence of the importance of Roman Catholicism in French life as well as the desire of the French to convert Native Americans to their faith. The French may have given the rings to the Indians as tokens of friendship and good will.

The evident quality of these goods led the archaeologists to think about the sophistication of the Native American peoples for whom they were intended, and to ponder the regard in which the French may have held them. Insistence on respect for the Native Americans very likely came from La Salle himself. Almost alone among the French explorers in the New World, La Salle sought to understand Native American languages and cultures. During his previous expeditions he had traded with a number of Native American tribes, such as the Shawnee. From that experience, he seemed to have acquired a certain admiration for them. In any event, La Salle knew that he needed to remain on amiable terms with the inhabitants of the regions he wished to explore and colonize. It did not pay to antagonize the Indians.

By late January 1997, the team had discovered in the forward cargo hold two more cannon, identical with the first one found in July. They also identified the imprint of a fourth cannon, which was missing. Truly, said one enthusiastic historian, this was a "most romantic find"—a treasure chest that spoke not only of everyday French colonial life, but of thrilling adventures as well.[29]

A Testament to Their Life

"The *Belle* was La Salle's last chance," concedes Robert Weddle, a historian who has devoted extensive study to the journeys of La Salle and to his time in Texas. "He could have never succeeded on the Texas coast without her."[30]

The importance of *La Belle*, then and now, cannot be overestimated. She was essential to the success of La Salle's venture. Three hundred years later, she has also provided archaeologists and historians with important insights into everything from seventeenth-century French shipbuilding techniques to their religious beliefs and their views of the Native Americans. More important, the little ship stands as a testament not only to La Salle's courage and accomplishments, but to the frequently overlooked history of French pioneers in the New World.

The archaeological team, now at work under a new project director, Dr. Jim Bruseth, has completed its excavation efforts. In addition to bringing more than 700,000 artifacts to the surface, the archeologists have disassembled the hull of *La Belle* and transported it to the Texas A & M University Nautical Conservation Laboratory for cleaning, preservation, and study. In the summer of 1998, construction began on a special concrete vat in which to house the remains of *La Belle*. Sixty feet long, twenty feet wide, and twelve feet deep, it is the largest conservation vat ever put into service for the preservation and protection of wood.

Like the cofferdam, the vat is a unique conservation tool. It will enable conservators to immerse, clean, preserve, and reconstruct the ship's fragile hull without endangering it. Attached to the vat is a metal frame with four motorized gearboxes. This frame will support the hull as it is cleaned and reassembled. When work on the hull is complete, conservators will use these gearboxes to lift the rebuilt ship out of the special liquid solution that is now helping to protect the wood.

By the end of 1999, the 764 individual pieces of the hull had been carefully placed into the vat where members of the conservation laboratory are now at work reassembling them. It will probably take between three and six years to preserve, restore, and evaluate every artifact, as well as the hull itself.[31]

In an exhibit that traveled throughout Texas during 1997, thousands of the artifacts taken from *La Belle* made their first appearance in more than three centuries. Plans are now being finalized to stage a major traveling exhibition of these objects throughout the United States and possibly also in Canada and France during the next few years. When the Texas Historical Commission team at last completes its study of *La Belle*, the ship and her relics will find a permanent home in a new state history museum. At present, the commission is evaluating possible sites on which this museum may be built.[32]

It has been a long journey for *La Belle*. Once the gift of an ambitious ruler to a loyal, brave, and resourceful subject, *La Belle* now serves as a remarkable time capsule recalling an age when the earth was a much larger and more mysterious place, when empires arose on distant shores in the name of God and king, and when men's dreams were not confined by their horizons.

III.

"Haven of Domestic Life": Slave Life at Monticello

"It is very central to [Monticello] . . . that everyone understand that this is not just a house. It's where enslaved African Americans lived and worked."
—Lucia C. Stanton, historian at Monticello, 1999

Thomas Jefferson is among the most admired of the Founding Fathers. He was the main author of the Declaration of Independence and enjoyed a long and illustrious political career. In 1800, Jefferson was elected the third president of the United States. Jefferson had many interests and talents besides politics and was an accomplished architect. His home, Monticello, is one of the finest examples of the Classical Revival style popular during the late 1700s and early 1800s.

Situated on a hill that rises to a height of 867 feet, Monticello offers a commanding view of the surrounding woods and farms of Virginia. The craggy peaks of the Blue Ridge Mountains hover in the distance. Modeled after a famous Roman temple known as the Pantheon, the house is a three-story red brick and wood structure. Projecting from the front is a large, covered portico, or porch, with a roof supported by classical columns. A striking octagonal dome, with distinctive round windows, tops the central block of the house. Jefferson's home is more modest than it appears at first, but it is an exquisite work of balance and symmetry. It is a testament to the rational, orderly mind that conceived it. Designing and building Monticello was the fulfillment of Jefferson's dream. He loved his home as he loved no other place on earth. "All my wishes," Jefferson declared, "end . . . where I hope my days will end, at Monticello."[1]

Today, Monticello is among the most renowned historic landmarks in the United States. Each year, thousands of visitors from around the world come to Monticello to learn about Jefferson's life and times. But is what they see a historically accurate depiction of the Monticello that existed in Jefferson's day?

Until recently, it was not. Before the 1960s, a visitor to Monticello would have toured a vastly different house and grounds than those Jefferson knew, and in most cases than he would have recognized. In 1960, one historian noted that the Monticello visitors saw "is not Monticello as it was in Jefferson's time, overrun with children and slaves . . . battered from daily use and showing the ravages of debt; but Monticello expertly restored . . . a fascinating museum, a shrine to Jefferson's memory."[2]

Jefferson did not build Monticello as a monument to himself, but as a home in which to dwell. Even more important, this house would never have existed if not for the labor of Jefferson's slaves. The plantation from which Jefferson drew most of his income would not have prospered without the African Americans who also made their home there. During his visit in 1796, the French Duke de la Rochefoucauld-Liancourt noted how indispensable the slaves were to Jefferson:

> Every article is made on his farm: his negroes [sic] are cabinet-makers, carpenters, masons, bricklayers, smiths, etc. The children he employs in a nail factory which yields already a considerable profit. He animates them by rewards and distinctions.[3]

At one time, Jefferson owned as many as 150 slaves.[4] As essential as they were to the daily life of the plantation, historians for years did not devote much attention to learning about their lives and work, though many wondered how a man who had written so eloquently about freedom could justify keeping slaves at all. After the Thomas Jefferson Foundation purchased Monticello in 1923, the primary focus remained on Jefferson's life at Monticello and on the house and grounds themselves. Tours and official publications gave scant attention to the slaves.

Any evidence of their lives, if visible at all, remained in the background.

Early archaeological excavations on the site were directed toward finding out more information about Jefferson and his family than about the slaves. Any information about the African American community that came to light as a result of these efforts was incidental to their main focus. Part of the reason for ignoring slaves and slave life was the apparent lack of written records. But the truth of the matter was that for a long time few historians and archaeologists were interested in African American history and culture. That attitude began to change in the 1950s with the emergence of the Civil Rights Movement. By the 1960s, a new generation of scholars had begun to investigate the African American past with greater enthusiasm and care.

Influenced by this new scholarship, the archaeologists who studied Monticello had, by the 1970s, begun to cast a wider net. Although Jefferson remained of great interest to them, they also started to explore other aspects of Monticello's history. In particular, the archaeologists became curious about the slaves and the community they had created at Monticello known as "Mulberry Row." Over time, these efforts yielded a rich vein of information about the black inhabitants of Monticello and their complicated relations with their master.

Central Virginia, 1763
Jefferson's "Little Mountain"

It was a priceless gift. In honor of his son Thomas's twentieth birthday, Peter Jefferson bequeathed to him approximately 5,000 acres in central Virginia. The land, located in the foothills of the Blue Ridge Mountains near the future town of Charlottesville, would become the site of Thomas Jefferson's plantation Monticello, which means "Little Mountain" in Italian. Beginning in 1767, and continuing until his death in 1826, Monticello occupied most of Jefferson's spare time and creative energy, to say nothing of his income.

Monticello didn't merely provide a home for Jefferson, though he

An aerial view of Monticello taken in 1995. Mulberry Row is the tree-lined path located to the right of the main house. The white domes on the house were restored to their original gray in 1993. Courtesy of Monticello/Thomas Jefferson Foundation, Inc.

built a magnificent house on the grounds. It was a working farm and a living laboratory, where he experimented with agricultural methods and machines and tinkered with building and construction techniques. Jefferson also tried to make a living from the various enterprises conducted at his mountain retreat, among them farming, operating a nail factory, and running a gristmill.

Jefferson could not have succeeded alone. To help with every conceivable task, including planting and harvesting crops, making bricks, building stables, cooking, sewing, and gardening, Jefferson relied on those whom he called "his people," by which, of course, he meant the slaves.[5] There is no doubt that without slavery Monticello would never have become a successful plantation. The labor of slaves was essential to the creation of the grand mountaintop paradise that Jefferson envisioned, for he could not have afforded to pay for the labor of free workers.

Monticello, 1979
"A Sort of Complex Kaleidoscope"

Dr. William Kelso, director of archaeology at Monticello from 1979 until 1993, believes "the past is a current event. The structure of it may be lost, but it is not unrecoverable."[6] Given his ideas about history, Kelso faced a big task. He wondered what historical archaeology could reveal about the life and world of Thomas Jefferson that wasn't already known. Jefferson himself had left a detailed record of life at Monticello. During the course of his life he wrote more than 20,000 letters and kept five journals. Yet he had said little about the daily routines of his slaves.

Kelso recognized that there was a great deal to be learned about the slave community at Monticello. He wondered how much evidence had survived and what it could teach archaeologists and historians. What contributions to life at Monticello had the slaves, in fact, made? How important was their presence? How did they live? What was the nature of their relations with Jefferson and with each other? Was Mulberry Row typical of the slave communities at other large plantations in the

Virginia upcountry during the late eighteenth and early nineteenth centuries? These were lines of inquiry that Dr. Kelso wanted to pursue, and he resolved to uncover every scrap of new information that he could find.

For Kelso, that effort required not only a reconsideration of the historical record, but the careful plotting and digging of the Monticello landscape as well. The objects that lay buried beneath the surface of the earth, he reasoned, might be just as important as the information men and women had written down. Beginning in 1980, therefore, Kelso and the team of archaeologists he had assembled worked diligently to discover the secret history of Jefferson's plantation. They were not disappointed. Kelso and the research team unearthed new and valuable information about the community of African American house slaves and craftsmen that had taken root and grown at Mulberry Row. These archeological findings fundamentally changed our understanding of life at Monticello, transforming it from a historic monument to Thomas Jefferson into what Kelso characterized as "a sort of complex kaleidoscope, . . . an interdependent community of blacks, whites, and people of mixed color."[7]

Monticello, Virginia, circa 1802–1822
Mr. Jefferson and His People

"Mr. Jefferson was always very kind and indulgent to his servants."[8] So begins a chapter of Captain Edmund Bacon's memoir, *Jefferson at Monticello: The Private Life of Thomas Jefferson*, published in 1851. Bacon offered a unique perspective on daily life at Monticello, having served as the plantation overseer for twenty years, from 1802 to 1822. An overseer was an important employee on almost every large plantation in the South. It was his responsibility to make sure the slaves performed their assigned tasks, so that the daily operation of the plantation was as efficient and productive as possible. Because of his charge, the overseer was often familiar with the inner workings of the plantation. Edmund Bacon had many opportunities to observe Jefferson's interactions with, and treatment of, his slaves, and to learn about their attitudes toward the master.

According to Captain Bacon, Jefferson did not overwork his slaves and rarely had them whipped or punished. He seemed to treat his slaves with the utmost kindness, consideration, and generosity. Jefferson maintained a large number of house slaves, who often received special treatment from him and the members of his immediate family.[9] House slaves served as butlers, maids, valets, and cooks, and performed other household tasks as needed. Unlike some prominent Virginia slave owners, however, including George Washington and Jefferson's cousin, the famous statesman John Randolph, Jefferson never made provisions to free his slaves after his death. Nevertheless, he granted some of them a remarkable degree of personal independence while he was the master of Monticello. Certain house servants, such as Burwell, remained at Monticello when Jefferson departed for Washington to assume his political duties. So complete was Jefferson's trust in Burwell's loyalty and judgment that he informed Captain Bacon to permit Burwell to take

> charge of the meat house, garden, &c, and [to keep] the premises in order. . . . Mr. Jefferson had the most perfect confidence in him. He told me not to be particular with him—to let him do pretty much as he pleased.[10]

When Jefferson began the construction of his plantation house in 1769, most of the fifty-two or so slaves he owned were field hands. To fulfill his dream of making Monticello totally self-sufficient, and to avoid paying the high cost of hiring local craftsmen, Jefferson encouraged his slaves to learn a trade. As a result, a higher-than-average number of slaves at Monticello became skilled laborers. John Hemings, for example, was a carpenter. Joe Fosset became a blacksmith, and the aforementioned Burwell, in addition to being a house servant, was also a painter. Other slaves learned to be bricklayers and coopers (barrel makers).

As on most large plantations, there was a distinct hierarchy within the slave community: House slaves were at the top, with skilled craftsmen next. The field hands and others with few or no skills were at the bottom. This hierarchy determined where slaves lived at Monticello, and in some cases influenced the amount of interaction they had with Jefferson.

Not long after he began construction of the main house, Jefferson also began to draw up plans for a series of buildings. These were to be built in the area known as Mulberry Row, so called because of the beautiful mulberry trees Jefferson had planted along the road. Located to the south of the main house, this area was connected to the rest of Monticello by a 1,000-foot-long cobblestone road lined with buildings on one side.[11]

Over time, this area grew to include not only the manufacturing center for Monticello, but also the living quarters for Jefferson's house slaves and many of the skilled slave craftsmen.[12] Here was the nucleus of the plantation, where slaves performed many of the chores necessary to the conduct of daily life.

Mulberry Row

In 1809, a friend of Jefferson's family named Margaret Bayard Smith came to Monticello for an extended visit. During her stay, Mrs. Smith made careful note of everything she saw. Among her many descriptions of Jefferson's "Haven of Domestic Life," as she called Monticello, was her account of Mulberry Row:

> It is in general shady, with openings through the trees for distant views. We passed the outhouses for slaves and workmen. They are all much better than I have seen on any other plantation, but to an eye unaccustomed to such sights, they appear poor and their cabins form a most unpleasant contrast with the place that rises so near them. Mr. J. has carpenters, cabinet-makers, painters, and blacksmiths and several other trades all within himself and finds these slaves excellent as workmen.[13]

As with almost everything he did, Jefferson kept detailed notes about the activities and buildings on Mulberry Row. Although he had contemplated a variety of designs for the slave housing he eventually built there, in the end he ordered the construction of four large dwellings made "of wood, with a wooden chimney, the floor earth."[14] These log homes, however, had few amenities as Jefferson provided little in the way of furniture, bedding, even cooking implements such as pots and pans. The dwellings could house as many as six adult slaves and their children. Sometimes a single family might occupy its own house. In fact, based on Jefferson's notes and drawings, Kelso concluded that during the first two or three decades of Monticello's existence, the slaves lived in large, barracks-type dwellings, and eventually moved into smaller single-family structures. The change in Jefferson's ideas about slave housing coincided with his return from France, where he had served for four years as American ambassador. When he came home to Monticello in 1789, Jefferson was full of ideas about how to improve his farm and the living quarters of his slaves.[15]

Along with the houses, Jefferson had a number of service buildings and shops constructed, including a carpenter's shop, a blacksmith's shop, a joinery (furniture-making shop), a nail manufactory, a stable, a storehouse, and a smokehouse that doubled as a dairy.[16] Periodically, the storehouse and smokehouse/dairy buildings were pressed into service as slave quarters, as needed.[17]

Approximately 200 feet south of the road running through Mulberry Row was a terraced stone wall that separated the houses from a large garden and an orchard. These provided fresh fruits and vegetables for all the residents and guests of Monticello.[18] The wall acted as a barrier between the garden, the orchard, and the slave quarters. It also absorbed and radiated the warmth of the sun and offered some protection against the cold wind, thus extending the growing season by anywhere from a few weeks to a few months.

Jefferson's precise descriptions of Mulberry Row give historians and archaeologists a clear picture of its appearance. But what was it like to live and work along Mulberry Row during Jefferson's time?

Depending on the season of the year, the workday could begin as early as four o'clock in the morning, when the plantation bell summoned the slaves to go about their appointed tasks. For some this meant walking to the main house to spend the day cooking or cleaning. For others it meant a shorter walk down the road to the nail manufactory, the wood shop, the blacksmith's shop, or the dairy. Mules clopped along Mulberry Row pulling wagons that picked up and delivered the materials necessary for the day's work. There were logs to burn in the kitchen stoves, charcoal to heat the forges of the nail manufactory and the blacksmith's shop, wood for use by the carpenters, the joiners, and the cabinetmakers. The pleasant smells of cooking, burning wood, and heated metal mixed with the more pungent aroma of animals and decomposing trash from the remnants of food and human waste. The voices of the slaves mingled with the sounds of hammers striking the forge, the pit saw cutting wood, and various animals honking, clucking, barking, and neighing. These were the scenes, smells, and sounds of daily life at Mulberry Row.

Monticello, Virginia, 1980
"Main Street, Monticello"

By the twentieth century, time, weather, and neglect had taken their toll on Monticello. What, if anything, was left of the area of Jefferson's plantation once known for its magnificent row of mulberry trees? It was up to Bill Kelso, the director of archaeology at Monticello, to find out, and to explain how Mulberry Row figured in the overall operation of the plantation economy.

Earlier archaeological excavations completed in 1957 and 1958 had uncovered some building sites, such as the joinery, nail manufactory, storehouse, and smokehouse/dairy. Those efforts were superficial, however, and little study had been done since. For the next twenty-one years, between 1958 and 1979, Mulberry Row was ignored and all but forgotten. Then in 1980, after a year of working at the plantation, Kelso was ready to focus on what he described as "Main Street, Monticello."[19] Based on Jefferson's precise description of the buildings, the earlier excavations of the 1950s, and the archeological work that his team had done during the previous year, Kelso prepared to reevaluate the significance of the Mulberry Row site.

The archaeologists consulted some written records to begin their investigation. Like many other landowners of his time, Jefferson had insured Monticello. To make certain the insurance policy was accurate, he created a precise map of all the buildings on the plantation. Mulberry Row was no exception. He mapped the locations of all the buildings and included detailed written descriptions of them as well. Jefferson noted that along Mulberry Row there existed nineteen buildings. He assigned each building a letter for easy identification.[20] Using the insurance policy issued by the Mutual Assurance Company in 1796 as a guide, the archaeologists went to work. Kelso and his colleagues relied on the relatively new technique of landscape archaeology to study Mulberry Row and its immediate environs. Many scholars, in fact, credit Kelso with inventing this type of archaeology as a result of the excavations conducted at Monticello.

When doing landscape archaeology, archaeologists sift through layer after layer of accumulated soil and study the artifacts they uncover in each one. At the same time, they note any changes in the various layers of soil. This slow and painstaking process enables them to date the remains, and even more important, to reconstruct the way the land looked at a particular time. Kelso and his team hoped to develop a sense of how Monticello must have appeared during Jefferson's lifetime and to determine the changes that had taken place since then. With this technique, Kelso explained, "even fragile signs of long vanished wooden fences or planting beds can be dated and recorded . . . [since] so much of what had been constructed during the first forty years of

Jefferson's development was changed at the time of or soon after his retirement from the presidency in 1809."[21]

The first significant discovery at the site was a long trench with holes. These were no ordinary holes. They were the original postholes belonging to a fence that had run among the buildings on Mulberry Row and helped to separate them from the garden terrace. In uncovering the fence line, Kelso and his team also located something even more exciting: the remains of a Mulberry Row slave dwelling.

"House O"

As the archaeologists found out, time had not been kind to Mulberry Row. Of the nineteen buildings Jefferson had noted on his map, only four survived above ground. These included the ruins of the joinery, a stone house, and portions of the stable. Another stone house had been pressed into use as an office by the staff of Monticello. The archaeologists wondered what might be awaiting them under the ground.

Using the map as a guide, Kelso and his team began to dig. Slowly, Mulberry Row yielded its treasures. It was as if the archaeologists had somehow brought the neighborhood back to life after more than two centuries of indifference. Not only did the team find evidence of the buildings that Jefferson had indicated on his 1796 map, they also discovered traces of structures predating it. All in all, the evidence pointed to a promising and exciting journey into the past.

The archaeologists determined that the remains of the slave dwelling they had unearthed belonged to a building marked "o" on the map. At first, all the archeologists located were the foundation walls, which had been constructed of stone. Centered on an interior foundation wall, the archaeologists identified a small rectangular brick box. It turned out to be a stone root cellar, which the residents had used to store foods such as potatoes and beets and also to propagate potatoes from one planting season to the next. Based on measurements of the foundation, Kelso and his team concluded that they had found one of the larger slave houses, which Jefferson had described as "a servant's house 20 1/2' x 12' of wood with a wooden chimney and earth floor."[22] By studying the concentrations of charcoal in the soil and a grouping of stones found nearby, the archaeologists determined where the chimneys had stood in the building that they now identified as "House o." The team speculated about what the slave quarters actually looked like based not only on Jefferson's description, but on a similar cabin located at a nearby plantation called "Bremo Recess."[23]

"House o" at Monticello, the archaeologists decided, was probably constructed of logs fitted together by V-shaped notches cut into the ends, which met to form the corners of the house. It was a single room with a stairway ascending to a loft, most likely used for sleeping. In front of the fireplace on the main floor was a small trapdoor leading to the root cellar. Dr. Kelso concluded from the evidence that although the buildings at Mulberry Row were small and simple in design, they were sturdily built.[24]

Further examination revealed an unexpected discovery about life in a log cabin with a wooden chimney. The team noticed a puzzling buildup of charcoal and nails at each end of the foundation. Chimneys in houses like the slave quarters at Monticello tended to be made entirely of wood, because wood was a cheaper building material than either brick or stone. The drawback, of course, was that wooden chimneys were more likely to catch fire than chimneys constructed of brick or stone. Kelso and the Monticello team surmised that fires were probably a perpetual fact of life for the residents of this home and the others like it. Yet they could find no evidence of the house ever having burned down. How was it possible for slaves to avoid destructive fires? And what accounted for the strange accumulation of charcoal and nails?

Kelso then remembered reading in interviews with former slaves about an ingenious aspect of the design of slave quarters similar to "House o." Wooden chimneys, supported by poles or props, were built to lean away from the main structure. When they caught fire, as they must have done fairly often, the residents of a dwelling had only to remove the props and allow the burning chimney to fall to the ground safely away from the house! The archaeologists determined that a series of chimney fires would eventually have caused the accumulation of high levels of charcoal in the soil. The numerous nail fragments resulted from the burning and rebuilding of the chimney after each fire. The way in which the chimney was constructed explained why only the chimneys and not the houses themselves had burned to the ground. To test their theory, the team built a house similar to the Mulberry Row cabin, set the chimney ablaze, and then let it fall, just as the slaves must have done more than a century and a half earlier. Their hypothesis proved correct: once removed, the chimney fell and burned a safe distance from the house.[25]

During the next several years, the Monticello team gradually uncovered the remains of five additional slave dwellings, all built in the 1790s. Three of the buildings corresponded to Jefferson's map as buildings "r," "s," and "t." By examining Jefferson's records, the archaeologists again determined what these buildings probably looked like. According to a 1792 account, Jefferson instructed his overseer to construct "log houses . . . at the places I have marked out of chestnut logs, hewed on two sides and split with the saw and dovetailed . . . to be covered and lofted with slabes [slabs]."[26] These homes were one-room structures covered with siding made out of wooden boards. Each one had a small clay chimney centered on the south wall. The homes were smaller in size than "House o," measuring twelve feet by fourteen feet, and they were generally more crudely built.

The archaeologists also uncovered what presumably was a two-room "negro quarter," measuring seventeen by thirty-four feet and probably built before buildings "r," "s," and "t." The remains of this building demonstrated to the archaeologists Jefferson's earlier preference for housing larger groups of slaves together.[27] Finally, with the help of Jefferson's descriptions and the archaeologists' measurements of the foundations,

Monticello archaeologists at the site of the excavated smokehouse/dairy (center background) and storehouse (lower right foreground) foundations. Mulberry Row is to the left. Courtesy of Monticello/Thomas Jefferson Foundation, Inc.

the team at last identified the remains of the storehouse and the smoke-house/dairy.[28]

Kelso's team was struck by another building that incorporated a different approach to architectural design. Instead of a traditional stone foundation and dirt floor, this building, which dated from sometime after 1820, rested on six brick piers. This suggested to the archaeologists that the building had a raised wooden floor. The team debated whether Jefferson was experimenting with a new type of house design recommended in agricultural journals during the early decades of the nineteenth century.

Slave dwellings such as those already excavated at Monticello had dirt floors and root cellars. Besides using the cellars to store food, the spaces were also used as refuse piles. Often, square pits, several feet deep, were dug. The trash, including food remains and household artifacts, was then discarded in these pits and covered over with dirt. Still, garbage had a way of accumulating beneath the house, creating an environment ripe for disease. Building homes with wood floors and then elevating them on piers allowed for the freer circulation of air and better ventilation. The improved ventilation broke down organic refuse more quickly, which made for healthier living conditions. For Jefferson, a healthier home meant healthier and, no doubt, more productive workers.[29] A photograph of Monticello taken in 1912 showed the house still standing, one of the few structures at Mulberry Row to survive intact into the twentieth century.

Communities on the Mountaintop

What conclusions about life on Mulberry Row did the archaeological team reach? For Bill Kelso, the individual artifacts uncovered at the site were interesting and important in themselves. But he still had to discover the relationship between those artifacts and others found closer to the main house. Only then would a more complete picture of life at Monticello begin to take shape.

Based on Jefferson's careful description of the typical slave diet, the

Monticello team knew that each adult slave received one peck (eight quarts) of cornmeal a week, one pound of pickled beef or pork, four salt herrings, and a gill (half a cup) of molasses. Had the slaves at Monticello relied solely on the meager fare their master provided, they would have lived at the level of mere subsistence. Like most planters, though, Jefferson never intended his slaves to survive only on the rations he provided. On the contrary, he encouraged them to supplement their diets by maintaining gardens, often on small plots near their houses, and by raising chickens or geese. In addition, during their free time, slaves could fish the nearby streams and ponds or hunt small game in the woods surrounding Monticello.[30]

Jefferson permitted his slaves to earn a little money of their own by doing extra work around the plantation or, if circumstances allowed, by hiring themselves out to one or another of his neighbors. Slaves skilled in carpentry, for instance, could make and sell furniture and other household items. Slave women who were expert seamstresses could repair clothing and on occasion could sell the clothing and quilts they had sewn. Finally, Jefferson encouraged his slaves to market the surplus produce of their gardens and permitted them to keep all the profits gained from these transactions.[31] With the extra money they earned, of course, Jefferson expected his slaves to contribute to the costs of their maintenance.

Among the articles found in the root cellars along and near Mulberry Row were shards of fine porcelain, tools, locks, nails, pieces of glass, buttons of all kinds, and bones from sheep, chickens, and pigs. By themselves these made for an interesting assortment of items. Kelso and his team wondered, though, how the slaves acquired such things. Their conclusion offers a provocative reevaluation of slave life at Monticello.

Kelso noted that many of the items found in the root cellars were similar to those discovered at other slave-quarter sites in Virginia, such as the plantations of Kingsmill and Littletown, both of which were located near Williamsburg. Excavations done at these sites unearthed a number of items in a series of uncovered root cellars.

Combining these artifacts with those found at Mulberry Row, Kelso concluded that the slaves' root cellars were used to store a variety of things in addition to foodstuffs and refuse. The various objects found in them probably came into the slaves' hands in a number of ways. They may have acquired some as the result of barter or as cast-offs from Jefferson and his family. It was possible, too, that the slaves picked through the master's trash pile and brought home articles that they could use in their own homes. A number of the artifacts might have belonged to white workers who on occasion stayed in the cabins while working at Monticello.

Kelso suggested, however, that the slaves might have stolen many of the dishes, nails, and other items discovered in the root cellars. Had these things come to them exclusively through barter or trade, Kelso believed there would have been a greater diversity from site to site. The similarity of items uncovered, though, raised the possibility of stolen goods being distributed throughout the slave community. That the slaves concealed animal bones (especially mutton, a delicacy for the master's table) provides one indication of theft. They could hardly have discarded the bones of stolen meat in plain sight. Kelso supposed, too, that the curious presence of locks among the artifacts was further evidence that theft took place at Monticello. Missing locks, which the slaves had concealed, would have made cabinets and storerooms more easily accessible to them.

Numerous historians of slavery have shown that theft was one of the more subtle and widespread forms of resistance to the master's authority and power. There was, of course, the added benefit of providing items that improved the slaves' quality of life. House slaves, and those who worked near the main house, would have had access to the cupboards, larder, smokehouse, and wine cellar that were often left unlocked during the day. If, as Kelso speculated, the slaves stole the locks, these storage areas would be open to all, until Jefferson got around to replacing them. Slaves could easily have made off with various foodstuffs, bottles of wine, china, and other goods. Tools that somehow mysteriously disappeared made for shorter workdays. Vegetables that vanished from the fields before they could be harvested for the master tasted uncommonly delicious.

There was nothing unusual about the theft of goods that most likely took place at Monticello; the slaves on other plantations did the same. Theft was a practical way for slaves to acquire what they otherwise would have had to do without. No doubt Jefferson knew what was happening. Instead of becoming angry, though, as did many of his slave-owning counterparts, he assumed a more philosophical stance and tried to understand the slaves' point of view. In a letter written to Dr. Edward Bancroft in 1788, Jefferson explained his thinking:

> A man's moral sense must be unusually strong, if slavery does not make him a thief, he who is permitted by law to have no property of his own, can with difficulty conceive that property is founded in anything but force.[32]

Alongside the household items and tools, the archaeologists found other articles that cast new light on the lost world and culture of the Monticello slaves. Here and there among the china, pottery, shards of glass, and nails lay an African cowry shell, some pierced coins, and a finger ring made from an animal's horn. These all pointed to the survival

Artifacts found at Mulberry Row reflect the slaves' African heritage. From clockwise: a cowry shell, Spanish silver coins, and a horn ring. The small holes drilled in the coins suggest that the slaves probably wore them for decoration. Courtesy of Monticello/Thomas Jefferson Foundation, Inc.

of elements of the slaves' African heritage. Until the late nineteenth century, many West African cultures used shells as currency. In some cases, these shells also held a religious significance and were sewn onto ceremonial dress. The team had no doubt that the ring they found was a *mojo*, a magic charm probably worn to ward off evil spirits. Rings of this type are still found in parts of the Caribbean. Pierced coins were a form of jewelry and were spiritually significant as well. The discovery of these artifacts gave a brief glimpse into what had previously been neglected or unknown aspects of African American life at Monticello. For Kelso, these findings demonstrated that elements of African folk and religious traditions had survived among the slaves living along Mulberry Row.[33]

The combination of the European and African artifacts impressed upon Kelso and his group that Monticello was a mix of cultures. From Kelso's point of view, the similarities between the artifacts found at the main house and those uncovered on Mulberry Row reflected "the closeness between the black and white communities on the mountaintop." More than that, the findings also revealed that, as Kelso put it, slavery was not the simple "institution that people too readily stereotype." If anything, the excavation of Mulberry Row, in conjunction with Jefferson's written record, demonstrates the complexity of slavery, slave life, and the relations between master and slave.[34]

Archaeologists are still at work uncovering evidence from the Mulberry Row site. In the last two years alone, they have discovered more than twenty additional slave quarters. The Jefferson Memorial Foundation has pledged $500,000 to complete the excavation and restoration of Mulberry Row, a process that promises to be painfully slow but well worth the effort. The archaeologists and historians now at work on the site also have an additional resource that ought to prove quite helpful. More than 600 descendants of the African American slaves who labored at Monticello have shared information with the teams trying to piece together life at Mulberry Row. As Daniel Jordan, historian of the foundation, stated: "We believe you can't understand Thomas Jefferson without understanding slavery, and you can't understand Monticello without understanding its African American community."[35]

William Kelso, who has since left the project, agrees. "I guess most people think of Jefferson as a super-hero, though to many African Americans, he was a super-villain who espoused both freedom and slavery," Kelso has said. "But these images do him a disservice by dehumanizing him."[36] From the ongoing process of excavation and the archaeological evidence already recovered from Mulberry Row, we can come to a better understanding of the intricate, perplexing, often contradictory, and very human world of Thomas Jefferson. He was surely the master of Monticello. Archaeology, though, has enabled us more fully to appreciate the African American slaves who were an integral part of this world and without whose labor Jefferson's dream would have come to nothing.

Like Jefferson, these men and women were complex human beings. Although they were the property of their master, they resisted the full weight of his authority over them. Despite their enslavement, they built and sustained a semi-independent community and culture that bound them together in their plight but that, at the same time, enabled them to hope for better days to come.

IV.

A Message for the Living:
The Battle of the Little Bighorn

"Those wasichus *had come to kill our mothers and fathers and us,
and it was our country. . . . The soldiers were very foolish to do this."*
—Black Elk, Oglala holy man, 1931

*"The physical evidence supports the Native American
testimony much better than the Army's testimony."*
—Douglas Scott, archaeologist, 1983

The battlefield occupies only a small portion of southeastern Montana, halfway between Billings and the Wyoming border, but it is associated with one of the most famous and controversial battles in all of American history. Although many Americans today may not understand exactly what took place there, most know the outcome. On June 25, 1876, Lieutenant Colonel George Armstrong Custer, in command of the Seventh Cavalry of the United States Army, died along with more than 200[1] of his men at the hands of Cheyenne and Sioux warriors. Five companies were wiped out in a single afternoon. The event stunned a nation in the midst of celebrating its one hundredth anniversary, and made the battle of the Little Bighorn a rallying cry to "tame" the Plains Indians once and for all.

In the years since the battle, heated debates have simmered over what actually happened on that warm Sunday afternoon. For many white Americans, the battle of the Little Bighorn was a heroic struggle that pitted skilled and brave soldiers against numerous and savage enemies. According to this version of the story, Custer was a great hero and martyr who was killed in the line of duty. Students of the battle traditionally pointed out that there were no survivors. But, in fact, there were hundreds of them. They were Native Americans. For years, however, their testimony was largely discounted, in part because their accounts were often contradictory and also because many people did not want to believe that the Native Americans were telling the truth about the battle. It has taken time for scholars to reexamine with greater impartiality and care the Native American side of the story. In addition, newly unearthed archaeological evidence points to a much-needed reinterpretation of "Custer's Last Stand."

A popular lithograph from 1926 shows Custer and his men surrounded by Sioux warriors. Romantic and idealized depictions of the battle persisted well into the twentieth century. Photo courtesy of Denver Public Library Western History Department.

Little Bighorn, Montana Territory, June 27, 1876
"A Bleak [and] Dreary Place"

The Wolf, or Little Chetish, Mountains stand between the valleys of the Rosebud and the Little Bighorn rivers in what is now southeastern Montana. These are not really mountains in the sense of the great Rockies farther to the south, but rather more like rough, carved blocks of hard ground that survived the erosion of prairie winds, water, and time. Sharp, craggy hills bump against deep, narrow gulches all the way to the Little Bighorn River. On the opposite side of the river is a broad valley of sprawling grasslands, spotted here and there with groves of cottonwood trees.[2]

To young Private William O. Taylor, this was a desolate, "bleak [and] dreary place."[3] He was riding with the remnants of the Seventh Cavalry just two days after the battle of the Little Bighorn, in which the battalion had engaged in some of the bloodiest fighting it had ever encountered. Taylor felt, as he later wrote, that "The Death Angel was very near."[4] Taylor and his companions were the lucky ones. They had been with Major Marcus Reno and had survived a bloody thirty-six-hour encounter with the enemy. Not more than a mile and a half away, Lieutenant Colonel Custer and more than 200 of Taylor's comrades had ridden away with the "Death Angel." In his journal, Taylor left a haunting description of the battleground:

> Our errand now was to seek our comrades who had died with Custer and pay our last respects. . . . After riding a short distance north . . . we came to an elevation from which a part of the battlefield could be seen. A bleak, dreary, place where, aside from a little coarse grass, nothing grew but an abundance of wild sage and a variety of cactus called prickly pear. Over it there seemed to hang an atmosphere of sadness and desolation, and little wonder that there was, for from every body on that bloody field but a few hours before had gone forth in vain most anxious

looks and prayers for our appearance which would have meant so much, the salvation of so many lives.[5]

Today was not going to be easy for Taylor and the other survivors. They were here to gather up and bury the dead before returning to Fort Abraham Lincoln in the Dakota Territory.

The Little Bighorn Battlefield, August 1983
"If the Dead Could Only Speak"

Summer had been unspeakably hot and dry. The area around the Custer Battlefield Monument, as the battlefield was then known, was parched: the vegetation was brown and dying, and the ground was cracking in places from lack of moisture.[6]

No one is quite sure how the fire got started. More than likely, it began when someone carelessly tossed a cigarette from a passing car. At first, the fire had spread slowly. Gradually, though, with the help of a wind that blew hot, dry, and dusty across the plain, a few smoldering sparks gathered momentum. Soon the Deep Ravine, one of the last points between the Little Bighorn River and Last Stand Hill, where the battle had raged, was engulfed in flames. The wildfire cut through the thick sagebrush, grass, and cactus that still covered the battleground, just as Private Taylor had observed more than a century earlier. Eventually four-fifths, or 80 percent, of the site's 760 acres were aflame.[7]

One of the many historians who studied the battle of the Little Bighorn lamented, "Oh, if the dead could only speak once!"[8] He, like so many others, still pondered the many unanswered questions about what exactly had occurred on the battlefield that hot summer day so many years ago. Where were the men positioned? Exactly how did the battle progress that afternoon? Did the many marble markers on the battlefield accurately identify the spots where Custer's soldiers had fallen? What were the movements of the Native American warriors during the battle? How trustworthy were the various accounts given by Indian warriors? Whether an accident of nature, an act of carelessness, or the will of divine providence, the fire that swept across the site of the battle created an unanticipated opportunity for the earth at last to yield its secrets and for the dead to tell their stories.

Little Bighorn, Montana Territory, June 25, 1876
"Otoe Sioux! Otoe Sioux!"

On Sunday morning, June 25, the sun shone like a bright yellow disk in the blue, cloudless sky. The wind was dry, and the trails that ran throughout the valley were thick with dust. High up in Wolf Mountain Divide three men stood taking in the view of the Little Bighorn Basin.

They were not admiring the sweeping vista below them. These were Crow and Arikara scouts in the employ of the U.S. Army, and they were tracking the movements of Sioux and Cheyenne warriors. Until now, the scouts were fairly satisfied that their presence, along with that of the main body of the Seventh Cavalry some miles back, had gone undetected. But that all changed in an instant when a small detachment from the Seventh killed a young Hunkpapa Sioux boy and chased away two others. The scouts knew the situation had altered dramatically, and that they needed to report this incident as quickly as possible to the "soldier-chief," Lieutenant Colonel Custer. The army had lost any chance it might have had to surprise the Sioux and the Cheyenne. They would soon know the soldiers were coming.

The loss of the element of surprise deeply troubled the scouts. Earlier that morning, they had sighted smoke rising from what appeared to be a large Indian encampment a dozen or so miles away from where they now stood. They had also spotted several Sioux ponies grazing south of the camp. One scout suggested that there were more Sioux in the camp than Custer's soldiers had cartridges! This made the scouts more nervous still.[9]

Upon their return to camp, the scouts reported their findings. One of their number, a cavalry scout and interpreter named Mitch Boyer who was of French and Sioux descent, said it was by far the largest group of Indians gathered in one place that he had seen in thirty years. Privately, Boyer confided to Lieutenant Edward S. Godfrey, "I can tell you we are going to have a . . . big fight." Another scout was heard to mutter, *"Otoe Sioux! Otoe Sioux!"* ("Too many Sioux! Too many Sioux!").[10]

The scouts' report did not convince Custer. A stubborn skepticism seems to have been part of his character. He rarely heeded the advice of others, and insisted on doing things his own way. And why not? He had often proved his critics wrong. His daring cavalry charges during the Civil War had made the phrase "Custer's Luck" synonymous with reckless but successful military exploits. Despite the grumbling of his superiors, Custer's daring earned him a field promotion to the wartime rank of brevet general. This advancement made Custer, at the age of twenty-five, the youngest man ever to earn the rank of general during wartime.

After the war, Custer, now holding the peacetime rank of lieutenant colonel, continued to make a name for himself. He was considered one of the bravest and best Indian fighters in the United States Army. Known to Native Americans alternately as "Yellow Hair," a reference to his long blond hair, or "Son of the Morning Star," Custer quickly rose to national prominence. No doubt the accounts of his exploits published in popular magazines, many of which he had written himself, boosted his growing reputation. Yet Custer's apparent lack of regard for his own life, and those of the men who served under him, made many of his fellow soldiers wary. Sooner or later, they reasoned, his famous luck would run out.

At this moment, Custer was embarking on one of the most important campaigns of his career. This was no simple scouting expedition, but one of the greatest military operations ever undertaken by the U.S. government against the Plains Indians. A year earlier, the government had ordered all the Sioux nations back to the reservations that had been established for them. Those who refused to go, the government deemed "hostile." Custer's orders were explicit:

As soon as your regiment can be made ready for the march, you proceed . . . in pursuit of Indians whose trail was discovered by Major Reno. . . . It is, of course, impossible to give you any definite instructions in regard to this movement. . . . The Department Commander places too much confidence in your zeal, energy, and ability to impose upon you precise orders which might hamper your action when nearly in contact with the enemy. . . . You should proceed up the Rosebud [River] until you ascertain definitely the direction in which the trail above spoken of leads. Should it be found . . . to turn toward the Little Horn, you should still proceed southward . . . and then turn toward the Little Horn, feeling constantly, however, to your left, so as to preclude the possibility of escape of the Indians to the south or southeast by passing around your left flank.[11]

Custer and his men were one of three columns coming from three separate forts in the Dakota, Montana, and Wyoming territories, to round up the Sioux in the area of the Little Bighorn and force them back onto their reservations. Custer was instructed to meet force with force if the Sioux refused to go peacefully.

The relocation of the Sioux was vital to the policies of the U.S. government. The area around the Black Hills in Dakota Territory had been granted to the Sioux by the treaty of Fort Laramie, signed and ratified in 1868. According to the terms of that treaty, the land known as the Great Sioux Reservation had been promised to the Sioux "for as long as the grass was green and the sky was blue."[12] Due to a series of unforeseen events, however, the U.S. government now wished to modify this agreement. The existence of a treaty between the United States and the Sioux nation seemed to make no difference. The government now wanted the land it had promised would forever belong to the Indians and their descendants.

One of the reasons that government officials wanted to withdraw from the agreement was that gold had been discovered in the Black Hills. Once news of the gold strike leaked out, gold-hungry prospectors began quietly slipping onto Indian land. In 1874, the government sent Custer and a geological team to verify whether the gold even existed. From the Native American point of view, the news was not good: the geological survey of the region found that gold was indeed present on Indian land.

The Native Americans had dealt often enough with the federal government to know what this discovery meant, and they were predictably furious. Once again, the government was breaking its promise. This time it sought land that was *Paha Sapa*, or "sacred ground," to the Native Americans. Here the Indians of many nations laid to rest their dead, and they believed that the spirits of their loved ones moved among the craggy peaks and hills. Parts of this area were also important to the Indians because of the buffalo herds that grazed there. The Native Americans hunted buffalo, which provided food, hides for making clothing and shelter, and bones and teeth for fashioning tools, weapons, and jewelry. The buffalo was the mainstay of their existence.

Federal officials saw the matter differently. Once the army had removed the Sioux from these lands, the way would be open for whites to come not only to search for gold in the Black Hills but also to populate and settle the Dakota Territory. For Custer, the removal of the Sioux took on immense personal significance. If his campaign proved successful, there was no telling how it might benefit his career. Many suspected that Custer entertained secret ambitions of one day taking up residence in the White House. If he succeeded in relocating the Sioux, with or without violence, he would truly be a national hero. There was already a long line of military men in American history, including Andrew Jackson, William Henry Harrison, Zachary Taylor, Ulysses S. Grant, and, of course, George Washington, whose military accomplishments had elevated them to political greatness. Who was to say that the same would not happen to Custer? As it turned out, the Sioux put a sudden end to whatever political aspirations Custer might have entertained.

"You and I Are Going Home"

Although he thought the scouts had, either deliberately or by some mis-calculation, exaggerated the number of Sioux preparing to meet his force, Custer did not expect the Native Americans to give up without a fight. He therefore ordered his men to prepare for battle. The Seventh Cavalry, he said, would attack that afternoon and rout the Indians from their camp. Upon hearing this order, the scouts began to talk among themselves. When Custer asked what they were talking about, one of them replied, "We'll find enough Sioux to keep fighting for two or three days." At this remark, Custer smiled and said, "I guess we'll get through them in one day."[13]

Unhappy with Custer's decision, the scouts knew what they had to do. Shedding their dirty clothes, they prepared themselves for battle by winding eagle feathers into their hair and carefully applying war paint. As they worked, they sang war songs. One scout signaled toward the sun with his hands: "I shall not see you go down behind the hills tonight." They knew that Custer thought them cowards, but they had seen the hundreds of tepees and all those horses. The Sioux and their allies were fearless warriors. The scouts knew they were probably going to die.[14]

Watching their preparations, Custer walked over to the group. In his usual brusque manner he asked the one known as Half-Yellow Face, "Why are you doing this?" With Mitch Boyer interpreting, Half-Yellow Face, a Crow, looked Custer in the eye and said solemnly, "Because you and I are going home today—by a trail that is strange to both of us."[15]

A Short Wait

They numbered somewhere between 3,000 and 4,000. There were so many of them that their tepees stretched along the banks of the Powder River for more than three miles. They had come from all over and rep-resented many of the different nations that called the Great Plains home. Here were the Cheyenne, a few Arapahos, as well as the many dif-ferent nations of the Sioux: the Hunkpapa, the Teton, the Blackfoot, and the Oglala, to name just a few. All had gathered initially to hunt the buffalo and set up winter quarters. But now a greater task was at hand. They would defend themselves against the blue-coated soldiers who meant to herd them like cattle or kill them.

Only eight days earlier, while camping on the banks of the Rosebud River, warriors under the brave Oglala Sioux warrior Crazy Horse had won a great victory over the soldiers led by the man they called "Gray Fox," General George Crook. Yet Sitting Bull, the celebrated chief of the Hunkpapa Sioux, said that the greatest victory of all was still to come. "We are an island of Indians in a lake of whites," Sitting Bull had announced at one of the many meetings held among the various Indian leaders. He emphasized how important it was for the different nations to set aside old disputes and work together against a common enemy. "We must stand together," Sitting Bull declared, "or they will rub us out separately."[16] The nations heeded Sitting Bull's counsel and formed the grand alliance that now prepared to stand against Custer's divisions.

Little Bighorn Battlefield, 1983
The Data Is Still There

James Court, superintendent of the Custer Battlefield National Monument, surveyed the damage. The horrible brush fire had left behind scorched sagebrush and exposed earth. To Court, though, the fire may have been a blessing in disguise. Surely now that much of the vegetation that had covered the battleground was gone, it would be possible to reappraise the archaeological evidence the site had to offer. Could a new study answer the questions about the battle of the Little Bighorn that had plagued historians for decades?

Court knew whom to ask for an expert opinion. He called his neighbor, archaeologist Richard Fox, to evaluate the site. Fox leapt at this extraordinary opportunity. For the next ten days, Fox walked the charred battlefield, searching for the slightest evidence among the blackened crevices and valleys. At the end of his exploration, Fox gave

Court the answer he had been hoping to hear: The site merited further archaeological study based on the initial number and types of artifacts Fox had uncovered on the field.[17]

Court was elated. He had been trying for many years, without success, to increase public awareness of the battle and the battleground, and believed that a thorough archaeological investigation would yield important clues about the events of June 25, 1876.

Fox sought the help of Douglas D. Scott, Chief of the Rocky Mountain Division, Midwest Archaeological Center, a branch of the National Park Service. Scott, too, was excited by Fox's initial findings and proceeded to organize a two-year study concentrating on the archaeology of the battlefield. At last, the earth was about to reveal the secrets it had held for more than 120 years.

Little Bighorn, June 25, 1876
"We Will Have Met and Fought the Red Devils"

At approximately 12:15 on Sunday afternoon, General Custer and the men of the Seventh Cavalry crossed the divide lying between the Rosebud and Little Bighorn rivers. At a spot called the Crow's Nest, Custer split his command into three battalions: Captain Frederick Benteen was to lead three companies on a sweep to the south, and then come east of the Little Bighorn River, cutting off any potential escape route the Indians might seek. Major Marcus Reno was to conduct three additional companies down the south side of Ash Creek, cross the Little Bighorn, and attack the Indian camp from the south. Custer himself would move west with the remaining five companies, paralleling Reno's advance, in search of the other end of the Indian encampment.[18]

The day was unbearably hot. The temperature soared to almost 110 degrees Fahrenheit. The men were exhausted, having ridden nonstop through the night. Their attempts to make coffee earlier that morning at a nearby stream had ended in disappointment; the water tasted so awful that even the horses wouldn't drink it. The Crow and Arikara

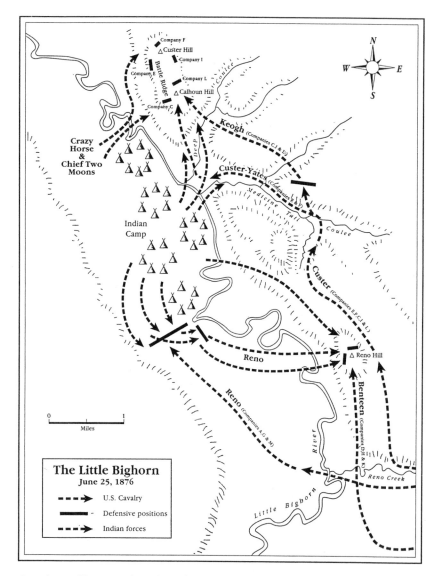

Custer's, Keogh's, Benteen's, and Reno's movements leading to the fateful meeting with Sioux and Cheyenne warriors are detailed in this map. Reno Creek is Ash Creek; Custer Hill is Last Stand Hill; and Deep Ravine lies between Last Stand Hill and the Little Bighorn River. ©Blackbirch Graphics, Inc. Used by permission.

guides, tired from their scouting expedition, talked quietly among themselves of Custer's foolishness in moving ahead with the attack.[19] Perhaps some were thinking of the dispatch that another interpreter had heard about. Newspaper reporter Mark Kellogg, known to the Native Americans as "Man-Who-Makes-the-Paper-Talk," was traveling with Custer and writing about the progress of his mission. Only the day before, Kellogg had sent another of his many dispatches to his editor at the *Bismarck Tribune*, predicting that "by the time this reaches you we will have met and fought the red devils. . . . I go with Custer and will be at the death."[20] The scouts found little to support Kellogg's optimistic outlook, and noted in any event that Kellogg had not said whose death he was about to witness.

Private Taylor provided the last description of Custer and his men going off to battle:

> His next, and final, appearance was on a high point of the bluffs overlooking the river and the Indian camps, a short distance below where Reno's command made their hurried and difficult descent. This occurred while Reno's Battalion was charging down the valley. . . . Custer was seen to wave his hat to the charging Battalion, a signal of encouragement.[21]

"Big Village, Be Quick. Bring Packs. P. S. Bring Pacs"

By three o'clock that afternoon, Major Reno and his men were engaged in heavy fighting with several bands of Indian warriors. In an effort to save his command and cover its retreat, Reno fell back across the Little Bighorn River and hoped to climb to the relative safety of the bluffs above it. The Indians followed Reno, engaging his men in bitter and ferocious fighting all the way to the bluffs, where they continued on the offensive. In the meantime, Custer, almost four miles away, prepared to attack the northern end of the Indian camp. He ordered Captain George W. Yates to take a group of men and follow him down the Medicine Tail

Coulee, a gully located slightly to the west of the troopers' original position. The remaining men, under the command of Captain Myles Keogh, were to be positioned on a ridge between the Medicine Tail Coulee and another gully, called the Deep Coulee.

When Custer realized the large number of Indians at the camp, he at last understood the danger of his position. He quickly dispatched a message through his adjutant, W. W. Cooke, to Captain Benteen: "Benteen, Come on," the urgent message began. "Big village, be quick, bring packs [ammunition]. P. S. bring pacs [sic]."[22] It was the last communication from Custer's doomed battalion.

Upon receiving these new orders, Benteen immediately moved his men to link up with Reno's troops. He then intended to swing north to join Custer's men in the fighting. Some forty-five minutes later, Benteen and his troops met Reno atop the bluffs where Reno and his men were still engaged. The battle was so intense and the fighting so fierce that it would be two days before the soldiers managed to fend off all their attackers. By then it was too late to save Custer.

"Heap Sioux, Heap Sioux"

While Benteen was on his way to join Reno, one of Custer's Crow scouts, Curley, had managed to escape the fighting between Custer's men and the Sioux at Last Stand Hill by pretending to charge with the Sioux. He then turned his horse and made his way out of the ravine, galloping alongside the Little Bighorn River. There he met a steamboat, the *Far West*, which was a supply ship for the army. The captain of the steamer, Grant Marsh, saw an Indian "naked, armed and riding an Indian pony."[23] Marsh knew something was wrong, but since there was no one to interpret, Curley was forced to act out what had happened. Marsh later reported:

> He would grab his hair, pull it straight up, groan, and then
> make a motion to indicate scalping, but this was not definite

enough. . . . Finally he grabbed up a piece of paper and pencil. . . . He first drew a small circle and within it made dots . . . to represent soldiers. He next drew a much larger circle surrounding the first and between them drew a large number of dots, saying . . . "Heap Sioux, heap Sioux." This made matters clearer to the dull people, for they now understood that the soldiers had been surrounded.[24]

By 5:25 in the evening, the battle was over. From start to finish, it had lasted less than an hour and a half. Custer and his men had met their deaths at the hands of what has been estimated as more than 1,500 Indian warriors.

"The Soldiers Seemed Tired"

In later interviews, Native American witnesses spoke of what they had seen. Sioux Chief Joseph White Bull described the battlefield scene in an interview:

All the Indians were shooting, and [I] saw two soldiers fall from their horses. . . . The soldiers fired back from the saddle. Soon after, the white men halted. Some of them got off their horses to fight. By this time the Indians were all around the soldiers. . . . For a time all the soldiers stood together on the hill [near the future location of the monument] ringed in . . . dying bravely one by one as the Indians poured a hail of lead and arrows into their dwindling strength. . . . The soldiers seemed tired, but they fought to the end.[25]

Two other Native American witnesses reported that some troopers had committed suicide to avoid being captured and killed, though they later retracted these accounts. Although later official reports invariably stated that the soldiers had fought bravely and in an organized fashion, many of the Native Americans, by contrast, said that some soldiers simply fired their rifles into the air, while others had panicked and fled. There was no question that the battle was full of confusion, such as this description of Sioux Chief Red Horse shows:

> In front of soldiers, White Man Soldier Chief was riding horse with feet like snow. White Man Soldier Chief had long hair, big-brimmed hat, and deerskin clothes. White Man Soldier Chief had divided soldiers. . . . Different White Man Soldiers shot guns not many times. We Sioux charged in midst of white men soldiers. They scattered in confusion. Different White Man Soldiers became foolish. Many threw away guns and raised hands, saying "Sioux, make us prisoners." By custom, Sioux did not take one prisoner. Sioux killed all Different White Man Soldiers. None were left alive.[26]

On one issue, most Native American accounts agreed: Custer's soldiers fought bravely and to the best of their abilities, but there were just simply too many Indians.

Four of Custer's surviving Crow scouts stand near grave markers at the battlefield, circa 1880. Photo courtesy of Denver Public Library Western History Department.

Little Bighorn Battlefield, 1984–1985
To Make the Battleground Speak

The task ahead was a daunting one for the archaeologists. They had reviewed the eyewitness testimony about the battle collected by army officials from Native American witnesses and the surviving soldiers and officers of the Seventh Cavalry. There still was no clear picture of what had happened.

There were problems with the stories themselves. Many Native American accounts contradicted each other. Some may have been designed to tell interpreters what they supposedly wanted to hear. Other accounts, including Curley's, changed over time, and were thus dismissed by whites as lies. Ambitious reporters exaggerated their descriptions of the battle in an attempt to gain more publicity for themselves and banner headlines for their newspapers. Charges that witnesses were afraid to tell what had really taken place, or that their accounts were marred by faulty translations, only added to the confusion. In an effort to avoid unwanted controversy, the official reports put forth by the army further distorted the truth about the battle, absolving Custer and his command of guilt. Still, the archaeologists found the Native American testimonies useful. Despite their inconsistencies, many of the narratives had details in common that helped the archaeologists piece together events.

Amid this jumble of information, the archaeologists were not sure what awaited them as they set out to investigate the fire-scarred battlefield. After much debate and discussion, Fox and Scott, with the assistance of the Midwest Archaeological Center, developed a strategy for studying the battlefield. First, they planned to examine it in the same way that the police study a crime scene, through the careful accumulation of all the physical evidence they could find. Second, they would use an approach that archaeologists sometimes employ when studying ancient building sites. This would entail dividing the battlefield into grids, or sections. When collecting evidence, the team would record the grid in which the artifacts had been deposited. As they pieced together their findings, they hoped they would begin to see a pattern that would enable them to understand how events unfolded and come up with an accurate reconstruction of the battle.[27]

The archaeologists pinpointed three areas of the battlefield on which they sought to concentrate their initial efforts. First, they planned to conduct a survey of the entire field using metal detectors. The next phase of their study focused on a section known as the Deep Ravine. According to official reports, twenty-eight men died and were buried there, though accounts varied from anywhere between twenty to fifty men perishing at the ravine. Both Fox and Scott wanted to survey this area to check for human remains. The last stage of the project would be an excavation of the areas on which marble markers had been placed in 1890 to commemorate the spots where Custer's men had supposedly fallen.[28]

Here the archeologists encountered another problem. There were 251 markers on the field, but only about 210 men died with Custer. The archaeologists hoped that their excavations could identify more precisely which markers were accurate and which were not. All in all, Fox and Scott sought to clear up some perplexing questions about the battle of the Little Bighorn and its aftermath, including what types of weaponry the Indians had used, whether the soldiers moved and fought in an organized fashion, and where the men had died.

The Battleground Yields Its Treasures

Working in three teams, the group set out. Volunteers expert in the use of metal detectors began first. Walking about five yards apart, they canvassed the entire field. When they came upon a piece of metal buried in the ground, the detectors registered the find. The operators then immediately summoned a second team—the recovery team—to uncover and examine the artifact. Once they were satisfied that the object was important, members of the recovery team signaled for a third team—

the survey crew—to record the position of the artifact on a grid map of the battlefield. The survey crew also measured the depth at which the artifact had been found and, in some cases, noted its condition. Only after they had painstakingly recorded these preliminary details did the archaeologists at last extract the artifact from the ground.[29]

The battleground willingly yielded its treasures. Within the first year of the survey alone, the volunteers and archaeologists discovered and unearthed more than 2000 artifacts, among them buckles, straps, buttons, boots, spurs, remnants of clothing, coins, parts of weapons, and arrowheads. The teams even recovered a pocket watch and a wedding ring! The assortment also included some 300 human and 200 animal bones, many of them belonging to horses.[30]

The Evidence

The most important artifacts for Fox and Scott were the hundreds of spent cartridges and shell casings. By carefully noting their locations, they could chart the movements of both Custer's troops and the Sioux and Cheyenne warriors during the battle. In a few cases, the team even managed to follow the movements of an individual soldier or warrior across the battlefield.[31]

While examining these artifacts, Fox and Scott made a surprising discovery. According to traditional accounts of the battle, the Indians were not heavily armed with rifles when they engaged the Seventh Cavalry. The archeological findings, however, contradict this interpretation. The excavation of the battlefield showed that the Indians were heavily armed and, in fact, often carried better weapons than the troops. The regulation Springfield rifles that the soldiers used were powerful and accurate, but clumsy to load. The Sioux and Cheyenne warriors were equipped with guns of more than twenty-five different calibers. Many of these weapons were repeating rifles designed for rapid fire. The use of repeaters gave the Indians a distinct advantage over Custer's men. In time, the archaeologists concluded that about 375 of the warriors carried older muzzle-loading guns and single shot rifles, and about 192 of the Indians had repeating arms. The remaining warriors probably used bows and arrows, war clubs, and some older pistols and revolvers. Based on these findings, the archaeologists believe that Custer's men were outgunned by almost two to one.[32]

Another of the archaeologists' findings contradicted popular opinion about the battle. From the way the shell casings and cartridges were distributed around the battlefield sites, Fox and Scott concluded that the soldiers did not fight a controlled action when defending themselves. Many historians and Custer enthusiasts have long insisted that the men of the Seventh Cavalry maintained orderly skirmish lines while probing for an avenue of retreat. Richard Fox thought the evidence told a different story. Upon realizing the number of Indians massed against them, Custer's soldiers panicked and shot wildly in all directions. In many cases they disregarded the orders of their superiors to stand fast. There was, Fox concluded, little order to the battle. He guessed that the men, moving together in small clusters, tried to make their escape. Unfortunately, they were cut down "like buffalo," as one Sioux account of the battle relates.[33]

Another important disclosure was the lack of handgun shell casings found in the area of Last Stand Hill. Native American accounts generally agreed that Custer's men only used their Colt revolvers toward the end of the battle, when soldiers and Indians were often locked in hand-to-hand combat. Because there were so many Indians, the soldiers would not have had time to reload these weapons. As a result, there were fewer spent casings present here than in other parts of the battle-ground.[34]

Laying to Rest

The next two phases of the project were the search in the Deep Ravine for any human remains buried there, and the excavation of the areas around the marble markers. A systematic investigation of the ravine using metal detectors failed to turn up anything of significance except for a handful of scattered artifacts. For the next several years, archaeologists continued to examine the ravine. At one point, they discovered a part of the ravine that corresponded to earlier descriptions of a burial area, thought to be the final resting place of several soldiers' bodies. But by the early 1990s, the archaeologists concluded that for the time being they would suspend the search. Archaeologists plan on returning to the spot to conduct a more thorough investigation in the near future.[35]

Excavation around the burial markers proved more fruitful. Here the archaeologists found a variety of artifacts, including pieces of a uniform, the fragment of a human bone, and an array of weapons, all of which suggest that the markers had in fact been accurately placed where soldiers fell. The forty or so extra markers, which had at first puzzled archaeologists, turned out to be duplicates mistakenly placed to commemorate an individual already recognized by another plaque. Even though Custer's men were reburied in a mass grave marked by a giant granite obelisk on the site in 1881,[36] the archaeologists still found the partial remains of at least thirty-two persons in individual graves.[37]

Ironically, a single marker in the Deep Ravine led the archaeologists to numerous human bones and enough artifacts so that they could compile a composite of the memorialized soldier. Examining this data, the archaeologists speculated that the bones they had found belonged to a white male, approximately twenty-five years of age, who had stood about 5 feet 8 inches tall. Buttons recovered at the site indicate that he had been wearing a regulation uniform when he died. Bullet casings suggest that the soldier had been shot with a .44-caliber repeating rifle. The rib bones showed that he had been wounded in the chest. Whether this was the fatal wound was not immediately clear, for there was evidence that this unfortunate fellow had also been shot in the head with a Colt revolver. Finally, the soldier also suffered from knife wounds in the front and back of his body, and had his skull crushed by a heavy object, possibly an Indian war club.[38]

A leg bone is photographed and marked at the battlefield excavation site before it is taken to the lab for further study. Photo courtesy of Little Bighorn Battlefield National Monument/National Park Service.

To date, the archaeological excavation of the Little Bighorn battlefield has uncovered more than 5,000 artifacts. Tests, including forensic examinations of human remains and a closer analysis of weaponry, continue to provide answers about what happened during the battle of the Little Bighorn on that fateful day in June 1876. Analysis of the human remains, for instance, suggests that only 10 percent of Custer's men were actually killed in battle. Archaeologists believe that the majority of the soldiers lay wounded and helpless, and were finally killed by Indian warriors who moved through the battlefield at the end of the conflict.[39]

Already the patient work of the archaeologists has done a great deal to help historians reinterpret the battle and reevaluate its participants. Although a single button here, a spent cartridge there, or even a collection of human bones may not reveal much by itself, taken together they can illuminate aspects of one of the most intriguing and hotly debated battles of American history. But questions remain. Who, in the end, was responsible for the army's fiasco at the Little Bighorn? Was it Custer? Or were his junior officers at fault? Some of these questions will probably never be answered satisfactorily.

In his memoirs, Private Taylor complained that "sometimes after reading some of the stories of that affair, I am inclined to doubt if I was out there at all and [think] that I only dreamed that I was."[40] The evidence unearthed during the past fifteen years at last helps to quiet Private Taylor's lament. This new information indicates that Native American testimony about the battle, despite containing some inconsistencies and inaccuracies, holds up well to the extensive scrutiny of the archaeologists. In the years ahead, archaeological findings will no doubt further clarify our understanding of the battle of the Little Bighorn. If we are fortunate, perhaps those discoveries will also shed additional light on the deadly clash of white and Native American culture that took place on the Great Plains during the last quarter of the nineteenth century.

V.

Buttons, Bones, and the Organ-Grinder's Monkey: The Five Points Neighborhood

"This is the place, these narrow ways, diverting to the right and left, and reeking everywhere with dirt and filth."
—Charles Dickens, novelist, 1842

I t was one of the most infamous neighborhoods in New York City 150 years ago. Its very name sent shivers running up and down the spines of respectable men and women. For many, the area symbolized all that was wrong with urban life. Thoughtful people dared not venture there unless in the company of a policeman or two. Gangs with such colorful names as the Dead Rabbits, the Plug Uglies, and the Roach Guards contributed to the infamy of Five Points.

Can the history of Five Points be summarized only through its rough and violent street life, or is there something more to the story? A group of urban archaeologists proved that there is much more.

Five Points, New York City, 1842
New York's Mythic Slum

Located on the Lower East Side of New York City, the Five Points neighborhood received its name because it marked the place at which three streets—Orange, Cross, and Anthony—came together to form a "five-point" configuration. Pictures drawn of the neighborhood in the early nineteenth century show the wooden sidewalks crowded with people smoking, drinking, and leaning against lampposts. This depiction of life

An engraving from Valentine's Manual, *a popular guide to New York City published in the 1920s, promotes the myth of the rough character of the Five Points neighborhood.* Photo courtesy of U.S. General Services Administration.

in Five Points implied that these idlers were unemployed, or earned their livelihood from some disreputable activity. Either way, they were regarded as an unsavory and disruptive element in the life of the city.[1]

Five Points was not only well known for its nasty characters, but also for the notorious conditions in which they lived. On almost every street corner was a "grocery," or an establishment then known as a "grog shop," where liquor could be purchased. Lining the streets were the dilapidated gabled houses and tenements that were home for the majority of neighborhood residents. These apartment buildings, grouped around a cul-de-sac known as "Cow Bay," had exotic but often menacing nicknames such as "Jacob's Ladder," "Brickbat Mansion," and the "Gates of Hell." These epithets were familiar to the police, who were frequent visitors. One popular legend, still repeated today, is that many of the residents' homes were linked to one another by a series of underground tunnels, which made escape easier if the police happened to be in the area.[2]

In 1854, an anonymous writer provided one of the most graphic descriptions of Cow Bay and its tenement houses:

> If you would see Cow Bay, saturate your handkerchief with camphor, so that you can endure the horrid stench, and enter. Grope your way through the long narrow passage–turn to the right, up the dark and dangerous stairs; be careful where you place your feet . . . for it is more than one shoe-mouth deep of steaming filth.[3]

500 Pearl Street, Lower Manhattan, New York City, 1991
An Amazing Find

It had been decided. A federal courthouse would be built at Foley Square in lower Manhattan, near the spot where, a century before, the three main streets of Five Points had converged. The proposed construction site was to the southeast of the once infamous intersection, bounded by what had been Pearl and Worth streets and Park Row. In accordance with the National Historic Preservation Act of 1966 and with New York state law, however, a team of urban archaeologists had first to examine the area to determine whether it contained any artifacts of enduring historical value. Only after the archaeologists had completed their work and evaluated their findings could construction begin.

Before the excavation of Five Points could get underway, the archaeologists themselves needed to do some homework. Examining old maps of the city, they verified that the streets, businesses, and tenement houses that had once composed the neighborhoods of Five Points lay beneath a century of dirt, stone, and rubble. These deposits actually proved a blessing, for they had helped to protect and preserve the site, as did the paving over of the area at a later date to create a parking lot. Using backhoes and cranes, the archaeologists set to work to remove the layers of debris, blacktop, and concrete. Then they turned over the soil with shovels and trowels and calculated the age of the remains before moving on to the next layer.[4]

By the time the excavation ended, the archeologists had uncovered and studied fourteen original lots within the courthouse block. During the course of their work, the team located an array of foundation walls, courtyards, and cellars. They recovered nearly one million artifacts from a total of twenty-two brick-lined foundation walls, cisterns (wells), and privies (early bathrooms). Their discoveries yielded surprising results.[5]

Five Points, New York City, 1842
A Plunge into the Five Points

In his book *American Notes* Charles Dickens wrote:

> What place is this, to which the squalid street conducts us? A kind of square of leprous houses, some of which are attainable only by crazy wooden stairs without. What lies beyond this tottering flight of steps, that creak beneath our tread?—A miserable room, lighted by one dim candle and destitute of all comfort.[6]

The Five Points that Dickens described was, indeed, a horrendous place. Ironically, the area that was to become Five Points actually started out as a rural district that, in the years before the American Revolution, was home to some of the wealthiest families in the British North American colonies. Their beautiful estates overlooked green fields and rested on the shores of a seventy-acre-wide and sixty-four-feet-deep body of spring water known as the Fresh Water Pond.[7] It was an idyllic setting, where the wealthy could hunt and fish.

Gradually, though, a growing number of tanneries and slaughterhouses were constructed around the Fresh Water Pond. Within a decade, the wealthy residents had moved away and Fresh Water Pond was reduced to a foul, stinking swamp. In time, the area came to be described by one newspaper as:

An aerial view of Block 160, the site of the new federal courthouse and of the historic Five Points neighborhood. Photo courtesy of U.S. General Services Administration.

a shocking hole . . . foul with excrement, frog-spawn and rep-
tiles. It's like a fair everyday with whites and blacks, washing
their clothes, blankets, and things . . . sudds and filth are emptied into this pond.[8]

By 1803, the waters were so polluted from the waste these industries
generated that city officials ordered Fresh Water Pond to be filled in.
The buildings and homes that still stood in the area around the pond
began to sink into the mire![9] To make matters worse, in 1819, when the
city finally covered the open sewer that had been dug to collect runoff
rainwater, city engineers failed to install air traps. Now instead of a
"stinking open sewer," residents and businessmen had to contend with
a "stinking closed sewer," which made the area even more unattractive
to city residents.[10]

In 1817, the area was officially designated "Five Points" after the city
extended Anthony Street. By then, the character, and even the geogra-
phy, of the neighborhood had begun to change. The once grand and
spacious residences were subdivided into smaller apartments and fell
into the hands of absentee landlords who did not keep the buildings in
good repair. Eventually these structures deteriorated so badly that they
had to be torn down. In their place, landlords built tenements into
which scores of men, women, and children could be crammed. On the
shrinking lots, additional shops and small manufacturing establishments also began to appear. With grog shops on virtually every street
corner, it was only a matter of time before the neighborhood became
home to much "unseemly behaviour."[11]

Despite its disagreeable reputation, Five Points was a popular place
to visit. During the early nineteenth century, reporters in search of sen-
sational stories for their newspapers frequented its haunts. Residents of
New York's more elegant neighborhoods, looking for an exciting and
dangerous adventure, stepped from their carriages to tour the coarse and
seamy sights. One visitor was the famed frontiersman and Tennessee

congressman Davy Crockett. He recorded his impressions of the neighborhood in his book, *An Account of Colonel Crockett's Tour to the North and Down East*, published in 1835. Crockett's description provides yet another glimpse of Five Points:

> . . . in the midst of that great city we came to a place where five streets all come together; and from this it takes its name of "Five-points." The buildings are little, old, frame houses, and looked like some little country village. The houses all had cellars. . . . I do think I saw more drunk folks, men and women, that day than I have ever saw before. . . . I thought I would rather risque myself in an Indian fight than venture among these creatures of the night.[12]

Missionaries, priests, and reformers were also a part of the everyday neighborhood scene, as they worked to save the unfortunate from lives of poverty, crime, and degradation.[13]

Floods of People

For all its ills, the Five Points neighborhood was home to thousands of workers and to a great variety of tradesmen such as potters, tobacco processors, printers, tailors, and shoemakers. Many of the earliest residents were Irish immigrants recently arrived in the United States. In time, immigrants from countries such as Italy, Germany, and China flocked to Five Points. Crowded into housing meant for only one family, it was common to find as many as thirty, fifty, eighty, or one hundred people living in a single dwelling. By the middle of the nineteenth century, the neighborhood was the most densely populated one in the entire city.[14]

A typical day in Five Points was a spectacle to behold. Imagine streets clogged with wagons, pushcarts, horses, and people. People moving in or moving out had their household possessions piled high atop a wagon or scattered along the sidewalk and street. Parents sometimes carried both children and bundles underneath their arms, or hoisted them on top of their heads. Voices speaking languages from around the world filled the air, as did aromas from fruit vendors, butcher shops, fish markets, slaughterhouses, tanneries, and breweries.

By 1894, the Five Points neighborhood that Charles Dickens and Davy Crockett had visited had begun to disappear. Social reformers convinced New York City's government that the only way to combat crime, poverty, and vice was to get rid of the neighborhood that had for so long been a symbol of everything wrong with urban life. The city thus began a systematic program to demolish it and, by 1919, Five Points was nothing more than a memory.

New York City–1992
"Beyond the Prejudices"

"We're trying to get beyond the prejudices that have distorted previous accounts," said Dr. Rebecca Yamin of John Milner Associates, the chief archaeologist at work on the Five Points project. Dr. Yamin was explaining to a newspaper reporter the reasons for studying so carefully the artifacts unearthed during the recent archaeological dig. Although the artifacts themselves were certainly recognizable to everyone, Dr. Yamin wasn't sure exactly what story these various fragments would tell.[15]

The artifacts were nothing extraordinary if compared to the treasures taken from a sunken ship or the cartridges and weapons exhumed from a battlefield. The items archeologists had found at the Five Points site were everyday things: thimbles, marbles, bottles, pipes, and a tea set or two. Certainly, though, these were not the kinds of things that they had expected to find in a neighborhood with a reputation for crime and violence. Perhaps knives, blackjacks, playing cards, dice, liquor bottles, and a few human skeletons would be more fitting. But for Dr. Yamin, the ordinary objects provided valuable clues for understanding the daily lives of Five Points' residents, who were turning out to be a far more complex group than anyone had imagined.[16]

The findings suggested to Dr. Yamin that Five Points might have contained a surprising number of hard-working men and women and their families. The only way to know for sure was to take a closer look at the New York State census and the annual city directories, which listed residents by name, address, and occupation. Perhaps then she would know more about the inhabitants of Five Points.

A Visit to Pearl Street

Early in their investigation, the archaeologists learned that the courthouse block rested on top of three older city streets: Pearl, Baxter, and Chatham. The wood shanties and brick tenements that once lined these streets had either been demolished or had fallen down. Since the early 1960s, the area had been buried underneath a parking lot. Now, almost thirty years later, the lot was gone. The old privies, trash pits, and basements were at last exposed to bring forth the wonders that they held.[17]

During the course of their research, the archeologists matched some of the building remains they found with people who had lived on Pearl Street; in so doing, they managed to piece together a composite of everyday life in Five Points during the nineteenth century. The industrial block housing tanneries, potteries, and slaughterhouses had gradually given way to other businesses. By the late eighteenth and early nineteenth centuries, bakers, brewers, and cabinetmakers were now operating establishments along this street. The archaeologists concluded that not all the residents of Five Points were victims of poverty or engaged in criminal activity.[18] Tobias Hoffman provides an excellent case in point.

An immigrant from Germany, Hoffman was a baker. He lived with his family at 474 Pearl Street and worked at his shop, which was next door at 476 Pearl Street during the late eighteenth and early nineteenth centuries. The household artifacts that the archaeologists found in the family's wood-lined privy (which may have also been used as a trash pit) showed that Hoffman had been a fairly prosperous tradesman. The Hoffmans had set their dining room table with pieces of elegant Chinese

Archaeologists excavate the walls of an old tenement foundation. Photo courtesy of U.S. General Services Administration.

porcelain and delicate wine glasses with slender, twisted stems. The family drank from engraved glass tumblers embellished with garlands of flowers. Teatime was probably an everyday ceremony in the Hoffman household, since the archaeologists found different types of teaware made of ceramic, porcelain, and stoneware. Most likely some of the tea sets were for everyday use, while others were reserved for more festive occasions. They also uncovered a German-made porcelain pipe decorated with a fancy gold pattern that contrasted with the cobalt blue background. In addition, there were glass containers for snuff, ink, and perfume. The red earthenware mixing bowls, worn with use and age, probably came from Hoffman's bakery.[19]

Studying skeletal and food remnants, the archaeologists surmised that the Hoffmans must have raised chickens and pigs to supplement their diet. The family also appeared to have had house pets, as the remains of a cat and several birds indicated. All in all, the artifacts illustrated a family that not only enjoyed the basics of everyday life, but could afford a few luxuries as well.[20]

An Irish Household

In 1848, a five-story tenement was built at 472 Pearl Street to house Irish immigrants fleeing the Potato Famine. Here almost a hundred people had resided in mostly two-room apartments. The tenement's residents worked at a variety of occupations; they were shoemakers, food vendors, grocers, cigar makers, liquor merchants, and unskilled laborers. Two of the tenants operated saloons on the first floors of 472 and 474 Pearl Street. The second address was the Hoffmans' former home, which their son had sold to an absentee landlord after his parents' deaths.[21]

There were a number of single women who lived at 472 Pearl Street. Many of them were widows who rented out rooms in order to meet their expenses. Sometimes this meant taking in borders to live in an already-cramped apartment. Since many of these women also had children, the living conditions were crowded. According to the New York

City directory, some women in the neighborhood worked as seam-stresses and laundresses, while others earned money by doing piece-work for the many clothing manufacturers located in the area.[22]

In going through the trash pits in the backyard of the tenement, the archaeological team pieced together what life must have been like for newly arrived Irish immigrants in the neighborhood. The picture that was beginning to emerge was not at all in keeping with the popular depiction of life in Five Points.

Once again Dr. Yamin and the other the archaeologists were struck by items that seemed to be cherished family heirlooms, which their owners had undoubtedly carried with them from the Old World to their new homes. Remnants of tea sets manufactured in England suggested that teatime was either a continuation of a daily custom enjoyed in Ireland, or an attempt to imitate the manners of polite society. Still, the team was curious about how working-class families could afford what appeared to be costly items.

According to Steve Brighton, a ceramics expert working with the team, dishes, teacups, and teapots like those discovered at Five Points

The site of an old icehouse where a number of artifacts, embedded in the far wall, were recovered. Photo courtesy of U.S. General Services Administration.

were within the financial reach of most working-class families. They averaged in price anywhere from $10 for fancy dinnerware to $5 for a tea set. It was possible, too, that residents of Five Points might have purchased their dinner- and teaware at one of three crockery shops that were within walking distance of the Pearl Street tenement. They might even have received a discount if the owner of the shop were himself Irish.[23] Among the other objects the team uncovered were numerous kinds of bottles: some once held olive oil imported from Italy; others contained gin from Holland, perfume from France, and countless different medicines to combat coughs, skin diseases, infections, and stomach disorders. Karl Reinhard, a parasitologist working with Dr. Yamin's team, drew some interesting conclusions about the presence of diseases caused by parasites.

In examining the privy deposits, Reinhard found no evidence of parasites such as roundworms or tapeworms. Further examination of the animal bones suggested that the residents of Pearl Street cooked their meat dishes thoroughly, which prevented them from contracting trichinosis, an illness caused by ingesting uncooked or undercooked meat. But Dr. Reinhard did find evidence of whipworms and the *Ascaris* parasite, which are commonly present in contaminated food and water. The evidence, however, revealed that these parasites were far more prevalent in the archaeological remains from eighteenth-century households than from nineteenth-century Irish households. Why this was so became clear when the archaeologists discovered the remains of a plant, *Chenopodium ambrosiodes,* or Jerusalem Oak, in soil samples taken from the site. Residents probably grew the mint-like plant, which was used to control the spread of these parasites, either in pots or in patches near their homes. The presence of these plants, as well as the various types of patent medicine bottles found, proved to the archaeologists that many of the residents of Five Points apparently took care to prevent and treat outbreaks of disease as best they could.[24]

One Man's Home

The pile of artifacts and remains just kept growing larger and larger. Rags pulled out of old cesspools suggested that the women who labored at home as seamstresses or piece workers for garment businesses kept the shredded wool from old cloth known as "shoddy" to make clothes for themselves or their families. Old woolen strips pulled from cisterns and trash heaps could very well have been what was left of braided woolen rugs that were made from leftover cloth and had decorated many a wood floor. Among immigrants, rugs were great status symbols that meant they had achieved a higher standard of living.[25]

Other artifacts pointed to the care that some residents paid to decorating their apartments. Archaeologists found nineteen red earthenware flowerpots, adorned with scalloped edges, and their matching saucers. Decorative ceramic figures were also popular; fragments were found of a porcelain dog and of "Toby" jugs, which featured molded comic faces. The archaeologists got a glimpse into the lives of the children of Five Points when they discovered china cups with children's names printed on them, tiny tea sets, marbles, and dice. Clearly, life at Five Points, wretched as it may have been, was far more varied and dynamic for some of its residents than anyone would have guessed, given the neighborhood's reputation for poverty and crime.[26]

Buttons, Bones, and the Organ-Grinder's Monkey

On the Baxter Street side of the block, the team found additional evidence of a working-class neighborhood. Instead of Irish immigrants, this time Yamin and her team found names in the city directories that gave evidence of German, Jewish, Italian, and African American residents. The directory showed that a synagogue had once been located at 8 Baxter Street. An overwhelming number of the artifacts recovered, such as needles, pins, buttons, embroidery hooks, and thimbles of varying sizes were of the kind typically used by tailors. These artifacts all pointed to activity in the clothing trade.[27]

Archaeologists also found that the food remains on Baxter Street were slightly different from those in evidence on Pearl Street. Based on the different types of bones, team members concluded that the German residents preferred dishes of lamb over pork. In studying an area where Italian immigrants once lived, however, the archaeologists found evidence of shellfish and fish bones, which were important components of the traditional Italian diet.[28]

Another interesting discovery was the number of clay pipes found at Baxter and Pearl streets. Pipe smoking was a popular pastime among immigrant workingmen, and probably among some women, as well. Irish immigrants, in particular, became so associated with pipe smoking that political cartoonists of the day almost always depicted them smoking or holding pipes. During the excavation process, the archaeologists uncovered hundreds of clay pipes. But of greater interest and importance than the sheer number of pipes uncovered was their great variety.

Studying the pipes, the archaeologists concluded that they were a personal expression of their owners' attitudes, aspirations, and values, just like the different types of dishes, cups, or flowerpots. Pipes found at the Baxter Street site often depicted the American eagle and thirteen stars, patriotic symbols of the United States. Pipes uncovered at the Pearl Street site, however, favored images such as the shamrock, closely associated with Ireland. Included among the finds were some unusual, and probably very expensive, pipes. One such pipe featured a bowl carved in the shape of a jester's head.

What did the presence of so many different varieties of pipes reveal about the neighborhood residents who owned and smoked them? According to Paul Reckner, a pipe analyst working with Dr. Yamin's team, the pipes that featured patriotic American symbols could very well have been intended to show support for the trade union movement that was beginning to take shape in the United States. Reckner explained that "Somewhere in every culture, there's a place where politics, work life, and ethnicity meet." That junction of politics, work, and ethnicity in Five

Points came in the form of the pipe, whether it was a plain clay pipe or one of more elaborate design. Most important, says Reckner, the pipes illustrated how the residents of Five Points sought to identify and distinguish themselves in their new country.[29]

Certainly among the strangest discoveries was a monkey's skeleton in an old privy. By this time, the archaeologists had uncovered such a variety of animal bones—those of cows, sheep, pigs, chickens, dogs, cats, and rats—that the discovery of another animal ordinarily would not have excited comment. But to find the remains of a monkey was extraordinary. Calling on the expertise of two physical anthropologists, the team members learned that they had stumbled onto the first non-human remains of a primate ever recovered from a site in North America. The obvious question was: "What was a monkey doing in a New York City privy?"[30]

The most logical explanation provided a real slice of nineteenth-century working-class life. During the mid- to late nineteenth century, some Italian immigrants made their living as organ-grinders. These men would stand on street corners and play a small, mechanical musical instrument called a barrel organ. By turning a handle located at the side of the instrument, the organ-grinder rotated a small cylinder that pressed against metal strings or rods to produce a tune. Often, organ-grinders used small monkeys to "dance," do tricks, and collect money in a tin cup from amused passersby. The privy where the archaeologists found the monkey's skeleton was one evidently used by many of the Italian organ-grinders in the neighborhood. No doubt, the remains belonged to a monkey that had helped collect coins for his owner on nearby street corners. But how the monkey got into the privy will probably always remain a mystery.[31]

"Are We in the Right Place?"

Most of the artifacts that Dr. Yamin and the archaeological team found did not at all coincide with earlier assumptions about the Five Points neighborhood. "When we first began to evaluate these things," Yamin wrote, "we thought, 'Are we in the right place? Is this Five Points?'" If the neighborhood was as horrible as everyone had supposed it to be, there would have been little archaeological evidence to study. Instead, the team uncovered and examined thousands of artifacts of different descriptions. Yamin believed that what they had found signified that Five Points was a neighborhood of the "working-class, not the down and out. This does not look like an impoverished culture," she said.[32]

From the evidence amassed, Yamin and her archaeological team also determined that Five Points was composed of diverse cultures. Its residents worked at a variety of occupations, both skilled and unskilled. Some were married with children; others were single. Although they were working class, many found a little extra money to spend on amenities to decorate their homes, such as the flowerpots that graced windowsills in the spring. Residents could afford to indulge in a few personal luxuries, as the fancy tea sets and elegant pipes suggest.

Dr. Yamin agrees that the "archaeology of domestic trash" is not nearly as glamorous or exciting as uncovering artifacts from a daring crime or a great battle. But the artifacts found at Five Points are equally important to our understanding of American history. They reveal how we have lived. Dr. Yamin and her team showed that "Five Points was a working class neighborhood where newly arrived immigrants and native-born workers struggled to find their way."[33] The archaeological evidence that she and her team unearthed also reveals the determination of immigrants to survive and to make a home for themselves and their children in their adopted land. The artifacts found at Five Points are thus much more than mere buttons, bones, and the amazing organ-grinder's monkey. They are a part of us all, and they tell our story as a nation and a people.

Conclusion
Small Things Forgotten[*]

The nineteenth-century French writer and statesman Alexis de Tocqueville, who recorded his impressions of American politics and culture, once wrote that the democratic age he saw emerging in the United States during the early 1800s required a "new kind of politics"—politics that took account of the needs, interests, and influence of the great mass of ordinary people. De Tocqueville might have added that the coming age of democracy also required a new kind of history. It would no longer be possible for those who studied the past simply to concentrate on the words, deeds, accomplishments, and blunders of monarchs, aristocrats, generals, and diplomats. Historians would now have to pay attention to the lives of ordinary men and women.

To study "the common man" and "the common woman," however, has often been easier said than done, for these sorts of people do not as a rule leave behind much in the way of letters, diaries, and journals describing their lives and their world. Perhaps, though, it is not too much to say, by way of conclusion, that historical archaeology has helped to bridge the gap between the history documented in written sources and the lives of the anonymous masses. Each of the five episodes examined in this book reveal the many ways in which histori-

---

*From *In Small Things Forgotten: The Archaeology of Early American Life* by James Deetz.

cal archaeologists have revived the past and restored its life. In their efforts to recover, reconstruct, and reinvigorate the past by investigating everyday objects, it may be that historical archaeologists have fashioned a democratic history for a democratic age. They have shown, after all, that simple people are never simple, and they have demonstrated how much there is to learn from small things forgotten.

Notes

I. Mystery, Murder, and Mud: The Discovery of the Jamestown Fort

1. Allison O. Adams, "Kelso's Quest," *Emory Magazine* (autumn 1997). Available online at: http://www.emory.edu/EMORY_MAGAZINE/fall97/kelso.html.

2. William M. Kelso, Nicholas M. Luccketti, Beverly A. Straube, *Jamestown Rediscovery III* (Richmond, Va.: Association for the Preservation of Virginia Antiquities/Jamestown Rediscovery, 1997), p. 4.

3. Ibid. pp. 4-6.

4. Adams, "Kelso's Quest," p. 2.

5. "The London Council's Instructions given by way of Advice," Philip L. Barbour, ed., *The Jamestown Voyages Under the First Charter, 1606-1609, Volume I* (Cambridge: Hakluyt Society, Cambridge University Press, 1969), pp. 49-50.

6. Carl Bridenbaugh, *Jamestown, 1544-1699* (New York: Oxford University Press, 1980), p. 9; Association for the Preservation of Virginia Antiquities (APVA), "The Location at James Island," *Jamestown Rediscovery, 1997, 1998.* Available online at: http://www.apva.org/ngex/location.html.

7. Association for the Preservation of Virginia Antiquities, "The Location at James Island."

8. David B. Quinn, ed., *Observations Gathered Out of "A Discourse of the Plantation of the Southern Colony in Virginia by the English, 1606" written by the honorable gentleman, Master George Percy,"* (Charlottesville: University Press of Virginia, 1967), p. 15.

9. Barbour, *The Jamestown Voyages,* p. 78.

10. William M. Kelso, *Jamestown Rediscovery II: Search for 1607 James Fort* (Richmond, Va.: Association for the Preservation of Virginia Antiquities/Jamestown Rediscovery, 1996), p. 18.

11. Association for the Preservation of Virginia Antiquities, "The Location at James Island."

12. Carville V. Earle, "Evolution of a Tidewater Settlement System," in Thad W. Tate and David L. Ammerman, eds., *The Chesapeake in the Seventeenth Century* (New York: W. W. Norton & Company, 1980), p. 97.

13. Ibid., p. 99.

14. Philip L. Barbour, *The Complete Works of Captain John Smith, Volume I* (Chapel Hill: University of North Carolina Press, 1986), p. 206.

15. William M. Kelso, *Jamestown Rediscovery I: Search for 1607 James Fort,* (Richmond, Va.: Association for the Preservation of Virginia Antiquities/Jamestown Rediscovery, 1995), p. 7.

16. William Strachey, "[1610] A True Reportory" in Louis B. Wright's, *A Voyage to Virginia in 1609: Two Narratives*, (Charlottesville: Published for the Association for the Preservation of Virginia Antiquities, by the University Press of Virginia, 1964), pp. 63-64.

17. Ibid., pp. 79-81.

18-19. Adams "Kelso's Quest," p.5.

20. Kelso, *Jamestown Rediscovery I*, p. 13.

21. Ken Wood, "Sifting Through History for Real Jamestown Story." Available online at: http://www.sunnews.com/news/newsmaker/nm99/newsmakr/032599.html.

22. "Rediscovering Jamestown," *TIME Magazine for Kids*, March 27, 1998. Available online at: http://www.pathfinder.com/TFK/archive/032798/cover.html.

23. Ibid.

24. Adams, "Kelso's Quest," p. 3; "Rediscovering Jamestown," p. 2.

25. Adams, "Kelso's Quest," p. 1.

26. William M. Kelso, Nicholas M. Luccketti, Beverly A. Straube, *Jamestown Rediscovery IV* (Richmond, Va.: Association for the Preservation of Virginia Antiquities/Jamestown Rediscovery, 1998), pp.1-7; Kalpana Srinivasan, "Political Intrigue May Have Been Fatal in Early Jamestown," seattletimes.com, March 11, 1998. Available online at: http://www.seattletimes.com/news/nation-world/html/98/altjame_031198.html.

27. Adams, "Kelso's Quest," p. 2.

28. Kelso, et al., *Jamestown Rediscovery IV*, pp. 8-11.

29. Ibid., p. 24.

30. "Rediscovering Jamestown," p. 2.

31. "James Fort Found," *Archaeology*, 49, No. 6, (November/December 1996).

32. Kelso, *Jamestown Rediscovery II*, pp. 24-25.

33. Ibid.

34. Kelso, *Jamestown Rediscovery I*, p. 3.

35. Adams, "Kelso's Quest," p. 2.

II. The Search for La Salle: The Raising of *La Belle*

1. Pam Wheat, "The *Belle*: A Gift from Louis XIV," *Journeys: A Newsletter for Educators*, 1, no. 1, (Austin: Texas Historical Commission, 1996). Available online at: http://www.thc.state.tx.us/Journeys/FocusHome.html.

2. William C. Foster, ed., *The La Salle Expedition to Texas: The Journal of Henri Joutel, 1684-1687* (Austin: Texas State Historical Commission, 1998), p. 49.

3. David Roberts, "Sieur de La Salle's Fateful Landfall," *Smithsonian* Magazine (April 1997), p. 41.

4. Wheat, "The *Belle*."

5. Foster, *The La Salle Expedition*, p.49.

6. J. Barto Arnold III, "Mystery of Matagorda Bay: An Archaeological Discovery," from the 1998 Program of the Philosophical Society of Texas. Available online at: http://www.bitstreet.com/society/philosophical/95arnold.html.

7. Roberts, "Fateful Landfall," p. 41.

8. An astrolabe consists of a disk and a pointer, somewhat like the needle on a compass. In La Salle's time, mariners used it to make astronomical measurements to aid in navigation, especially the reckoning of latitude.

9. Francis Parkman, *La Salle and the Discovery of the Great West* from *France and England in North America: Volume One.* (New York: Literary Classics of the United States, 1983), p. 974.

10. Roberts, "Fateful Landfall," p. 45.

11. Foster, *The La Salle Expedition*, p. 66.

12. Roberts, "Fateful Landfall," pp. 41-42.

13. Roberts, "Fateful Landfall," p. 42; Texas Historical Commission, "Fate of the Belle," *The Medallion*, nd.

14. Ibid.

15. Foster, *The La Salle Expedition*, p. 135.

16. Ibid.

17. Texas Historical Commission, "Fate of the Belle."

18. Anka Muhlstein, *La Salle: Explorer of the North American Frontier* (New York: Arcade Publishing, 1994), p. 216.

19. Roberts, "Fateful Landfall," p. 43.

20. Texas Historical Commission, "Discovery of La Salle Shipwreck Hailed as Greatest Find in Decades," *The Medallion*, nd.

21-23. Roberts, "Fateful Landfall," p. 43.

24. Texas Historical Commission, "Cofferdam Fact Sheet," *The Medallion*, nd.

25. Dan Parker, "Raising the Belle," Available online at:
http://www.caller.com.newsarch/lasalle1.html; Roberts, "Fateful Landfall," pp. 44-46.

26. Roberts, "Fateful Landfall," p. 46.

27. J. Barto Arnold, III quoted in Parker, "Raising the Belle."

28. Roberts, "Fateful Landfall," p. 48; Parker, "Raising the Belle," np.

29. Ibid.

30. Roberts, "Fateful Landfall," p. 50.

31. Texas Historical Commission, "La Salle Shipwreck Artifacts Exhibit Fact Sheet," *The Medallion*, nd.

32. Ibid.

III. "Haven of Domestic Life": Slave Life at Monticello

1. Monticello web site. Available online at: http://www.monticello.org/Day/plantation.home.html.

2. Jack McLaughlin, *Jefferson and Monticello: The Biography of a Builder* (New York: Henry Holt and Company, 1988), p. 383.

3. Ibid., p. 112.

4. "To Labour for Another," from "A Day in the Life," Monticello web site. Available online at: http://www.monticello.org/Day/plantation.home.html.

5. McLaughlin, *Jefferson and Monticello*, p. 95.

6. Ken Wood, "Sifting Through History for Real Jamestown Story."

7. Richard A. Wertime, "The Landscape Genius," *Archaeology*, (May/June 1993), p. 53.

8. Reverend Hamilton Wilcox Pierson, *Jefferson at Monticello: The Private Life of Thomas Jefferson* from James A. Bear, Jr., ed., *Jefferson at Monticello: Recollection of a Slave and of a Monticello Overseer.* (Charlottesville: University Press of Virginia, 1995), p. 97.

9. McLaughlin, *Jefferson and Monticello*, p. 96.

10. Ibid., p. 99.

11. Monticello web site, "To Labour for Another."

12. McLaughlin, *Jefferson and Monticello*, p. 29.

13. Margaret Bayard Smith, "The Haven of Domestic Life," in Gaillard Hunt, ed., *The First Forty Years of Washington Society* (New York: Charles Scribner's Sons, 1906), p. 68.

14. Ibid., p. 144.

15. William M. Kelso, *Archaeology at Monticello* (Charlottesville, Va.: The Thomas Jefferson Memorial Foundation, 1997), pp. 66-67.

16. Ibid., p. 62.

17. Ibid., pp. 62-64.

18. Ibid.

19. Ibid., p. 13.

20. William M. Kelso, "Slave Life at Monticello," *Archaeology* (September/October 1986), p. 31.

21. McLaughlin, *Jefferson and Monticello*, p. 347.

22. Kelso, *Archaeology at Monticello*, p. 52.

23. Ibid., p. 54.

24. Ibid., pp. 55-56.

25. Ibid., p. 57.

26. Kelso, "Slave Life at Monticello," p. 34.

27. Ibid.

28. Ibid., p. 31.

29. Kelso, *Archaeology at Monticello*, p. 61.

30. Robert C. Baron, ed., *The Garden and Farm Books of Thomas Jefferson* (Golden, Colo.: Fulcrum Publishing, 1987), pp 272-73, 284, 288-91.

31. Kelso, *Archaeology at Monticello*, p. 68.

32. Ibid., p. 69.

33. Ibid., pp. 73-74.

34. Wertime, "The Landscape Genius," p. 53.

35. William R. Macklin, "The Other Side of Monticello." *philly.com*, May 19,1999. Available online at: http://www.philly.com/packages/history/life/america/hemings/JEFF19.asp.

36. Wertime, "The Landscape Genius," p. 53.

IV. A Message for the Living: The Battle of the Little Bighorn

1. The number of men killed under Custer varies from account to account. The National Park Service's official count places the toll at 216.

2. David Humphreys Miller, *Custer's Fall: The Native American Side of the Story* (New York: Meridian, 1985), p. 7.

3. William O. Taylor, *With Custer on the Little Bighorn*, (New York: Viking Press, 1996), p. 73.

4. Ibid., p. 35.

5. Ibid., p. 73.

6. The Custer Battlefield Monument was subsequently renamed the Little Bighorn Battlefield National Monument in 1992 by the National Park Service. It was renamed in order to recognize the Native Americans who also fought and died.

7. Douglas D. Scott and Melissa A. Connor, "Post-mortem at the Little Bighorn," *Natural History* (June 1986), p. 17.

8. Kenneth Hammer, ed., *Custer in '76: Walter Camp's Notes on the Custer Fight* (Salt Lake City, Utah: Brigham Young University Press, 1976), p. 263.

9. Miller, *Custer's Fall*, p. 8.

10. Edward S. Godfrey, "Custer's Last Battle," *Century* Magazine, (January 1892), pp. 358-87.

11. Hammer, *Custer in '76*, p. 257.

12. Scott and Conner, "Post-mortem," p. 19.

13. Miller, *Custer's Fall*, pp. 19-20.

14. Scott and Conner, "Post-mortem," p. 19.

15. Ibid.

16. Sheila Black, *Sitting Bull and the Battle of the Little Bighorn* (New York: Silver Burdette, 1989), p. 84.

17. Richard Allan Fox, Jr., *Archaeology, History, and Custer's Last Battle* (Norman: University of Oklahoma Press, 1993), Preface.

18. James Welch with Paul Stekler, *Killing Custer: The Battle of the Little Bighorn and the Fate of the Plains Indians* (New York: W. W. Norton & Company, 1994), p. 149.

19. Ibid., pp. 149-50.

20. Miller, *Custer's Fall*, p. 70.

21. Taylor, *With Custer*, p. 66.

22. Scott and Conner, "Post-mortem," p. 20.

23. Hammer, *Custer in '76*, pp. 159-60.

24. Ibid.

25. Stanley Vestal, "The Battle of Little Big Horn," in *The Custer Reader*, Paul Andrew Hutton, ed. (Lincoln: University of Nebraska Press, 1992), pp. 339-43.

26. Jessie Brewer McGaw, *Chief Red Horse Tells About Custer* (New York: Elsevier/Nelson Books, 1981), n.p.

27. Scott and Conner, "Post-mortem," p. 21.

28-32. Ibid., pp. 20-23.

33. Welch, *Killing Custer*, pp. 169-70.

34. Scott and Conner, "Post-mortem," pp. 24-25.

35. Sandy Barnard, *Shovels & Speculation: Archaeology Hunts Custer* (Terre Haute, Ind.: AST Press, 1990), p. 22.

36. In 1879, a congressional decree established Custer Battlefield National Cemetery. The soldiers, Native American scouts, and civilians who died at Little Bighorn were laid to rest there. Custer's body was returned to the East and buried at West Point, New York.

37. Scott and Conner, "Post-mortem," p. 25.

38. Ibid., p. 26.

39. Scott and Conner, "Post-mortem," p. 26; National Park Service "Myths of the Battle of Little Bighorn," available online at: http://www.nps.gov/libi/myths.html.

40. Taylor, *With Custer*, p. 2.

V. Buttons, Bones, and the Organ-Grinder's Monkey:
The Five Points Neighborhood

1. Luc Sante, *Low Life: Lures and Snares of Old New York* (New York: Farrar, Straus & Giroux, 1991), p. 28.

2. Ibid.

3. Ibid., pp. 28-29.

4. Rebecca Yamin, "New York's Mythic Slum," *Archaeology* (March/April 1997), p. 46.

5. Ibid.

6. Charles Dickens, *American Notes* (New York: St. Martin's Press, 1985), pp. 80-81.

7. "Slum Lore," *Village Voice*, January 1, 1996 (Volume 1, p. 34); Edwin G. Burrows and Mike Wallace, *Gotham: A History of New York City to 1898* (New York: Oxford University Press, 1999), p. 746.

8. Burrows and Wallace, *Gotham*, p. 359.

9. "Slum Lore," p. 34.

10. Burrows and Wallace, *Gotham*, p. 360.

11. "Slum Lore," p. 34.

12. Sante, *Low Life*, p. 292.

13. Ibid.

14. Burrows and Wallace, *Gotham*, p. 746.

15. "Slum Lore," p. 35.

16-23. Yamin, "New York's Mythic Slum," p. 47.

24. Ibid., p. 50.

25. Ibid.

26. Ibid., pp. 50-51.

27. Ibid.

28. Ibid., p. 52.

29. Yamin, "New York's Mythic Slum," p. 52; "Slum Lore," p. 37.

30. Pamela Crabtree and Claudia Milne, "Monkey in the Privy!," *Archaeology* (March/April 1997), p. 49.

31. Ibid.

32. "Slum Lore," p. 37.

33. Yamin, "New York's Mythic Slum," p. 53.

Bibliography

Adams, Allison O. "Kelso's Quest." *Emory Magazine* (autumn 1997). http://www.emory.edu/EMORY_MAGAZINE/fall97/kelso.html.

Arnold, J. Barto, III. "The Mystery of Matagorda Bay," from the 1998 Program of the Philosophical Society of Texas. http://www.bitstreet.com/society/philosophical/95arnold.html.

Association for the Preservation of Virginia Antiquities. "The Location at James Island," *Jamestown Rediscovery, 1997, 1998* http://www.apva.org/ngex/location.html.

Barbour, Philip L. *The Complete Works of Captain John Smith, Volume I.* Chapel Hill: University of North Carolina Press, 1986.

————. *The Jamestown Voyages Under the First Charter, 1606-1609.* Cambridge: Hakluyt Society, Cambridge University Press, 1969.

Barnard, Sandy. *Shovels & Speculation: Archaeology Hunts Custer.* Terre Haute, Ind.: AST Press, 1990.

Barnett, Louise. *Touched by Fire: The Life, Death, and Mythic Afterlife of George Armstrong Custer.* New York: Henry Holt and Company, 1996.

Baron, Robert C., ed. *The Garden and Farm Books of Thomas Jefferson.* Golden, Colo.: Fulcrum Publishing, 1987.

Bear, James A., Jr., ed. *Jefferson at Monticello: Recollections of a Monticello Slave and of a Monticello Overseer.* Charlottesville: University Press of Virginia, 1995.

Black Elk. *Black Elk Speaks: as Told to John Neihardt.* New York: MJF Books, 1972.

Black, Sheila. *Sitting Bull and the Battle of the Little Bighorn.* New York: Silver Burdette, 1989.

Bridenbaugh, Carl. *Jamestown, 1544-1699.* New York: Oxford University Press, 1980.

Burrows, Edwin G., and Mike Wallace. *Gotham: A History of New York City to 1898.* New York: Oxford University Press, 1999.

Connell, Evan S. *Son of the Morning Star: Custer and the Little Bighorn.* San Francisco: North Point Press, 1984.

Crabtree, Pamela and Claudia Milne. "Monkey in the Privy!" *Archaeology* (March/April 1997).

Deetz, James. *In Small Things Forgotten: The Archaeology of Early American Life.* New York: Anchor Books. 1977.

Dickens, Charles. *American Notes.* New York: St. Martin's Press, 1985.

Fagan, Brian. *Time Detectives: How Archaeologists Use Technology to Recapture the Past.* New York: Simon & Schuster, 1995.

Foster, William C., ed. *The La Salle Expedition to Texas: The Journal of Henri Joutel, 1684-1687.* Austin: Texas State Historical Commission, 1998.

Fox, Richard Allan, Jr. *Archaeology, History, and Custer's Last Battle.* Norman: University of Oklahoma Press, 1993.

———. "A New View of Custer's Last Battle." *American History Illustrated,* 28, no.4 (Sept./Oct. 1993).

Genovese, Eugene. *Roll, Jordan, Roll: The World the Slaves Made.* New York: Vintage, 1976.

Godfrey, Edward S. "Custer's Last Battle." *Century* (January 1892).

Hammer, Kenneth, ed. *Custer in '76: Walter Camp's Notes on the Custer Fight.* Salt Lake City, Utah: Brigham Young University Press, 1976.

Hantman, Jeffrey L. and Gary Dunham. "The Enlightened Archaeologist." *Archaeology* (May/June 1993).

Hume, Ivor Noel. *Historical Archaeology: A Comprehensive Guide.* New York: Alfred A. Knopf, 1969.

————. *The Virginia Adventure: Roanoke to James Towne: An Archaeological and Historical Odyssey.* Charlottesville: University Press of Virginia, 1994.

Hunt, Gaillard, ed. *The First Forty Years of Washington Society.* New York: Charles Scribner's Sons, 1906.

Hutton, Paul Andrew, ed. *The Custer Reader.* Lincoln: University of Nebraska Press, 1992. "James Fort Found." *Archaeology*, 49, no. 6, (November/December 1996).

Kelso, William M., *Archaeology at Monticello.* Charlottesville, Va.: The Thomas Jefferson Memorial Foundation, 1997.

————. "The Archaeology of Slave Life at Thomas Jefferson's Monticello: A Wolf by the Ears." *Journal of New World Archaeology.* 6, no. 4 (June 1986).

————. *Jamestown Rediscovery I: Search for 1607 James Fort.* Richmond, Va.: Association for the Preservation of Virginia Antiquities/ Jamestown Rediscovery, 1995.

————. *Jamestown Rediscovery II: Search for 1607 James Fort.* Richmond, Va.: Association for the Preservation of Virginia Antiquities/Jamestown Rediscovery, 1996.

————. "Slave Life at Monticello." *Archaeology* (September/October 1986).

Kelso, William M., Nicholas M. Luccketti, Beverly A. Straube. *Jamestown Rediscovery III*. Richmond, Va.: Association for the Preservation of Virginia Antiquities/Jamestown Rediscovery, 1997.

————. *Jamestown Rediscovery IV*. Richmond, Va.: Association for the Preservation of Virginia Antiquities/Jamestown Rediscovery, 1998.

McGaw, Jessie Brewer. *Chief Red Horse Tells About Custer*. New York: Elsevier/Nelson Books, 1981.

McLaughlin, Jack. *Jefferson and Monticello: The Biography of a Builder*. New York: Henry Holt and Company, 1988.

Macklin, William R. "The Other Side of Monticello." *philly.com*, May 19, 1999. http://www.philly.com/packages/history/life/america/hemings/JEFF19.asp.

Miller, David Humphreys. *Custer's Fall: The Native American Side of the Story*. New York: Meridian, 1985.

Muhlstein, Anka. *La Salle: Explorer of the North American Frontier*. New York: Arcade Publishing, 1994.

"Park Dig Yields Custer Artifacts." *National Parks*, (November/ December 1989).

Parker, Dan. "Raising the Belle." http://www.caller.com.newsarch/lasalle1.html.

Parkman, Francis. *France and England in North America: Volume One*. New York: Literary Classics of the United States, 1983.

Peden, William, ed. *Thomas Jefferson: Notes on the State of Virginia*. New York: W. W. Norton & Company, 1982.

Quinn, David B., ed. *Observations Gathered Out of "A Discourse of the Plantation of the Southern Colony in Virginia by the English, 1606" written by the honorable gentleman, Master George Percy*. Charlottesville: University of Virginia Press, 1967.

Randall, Willard Sterne. *Thomas Jefferson: A Life*. New York: Henry Holt and Company, 1993.

"Rediscovering Jamestown." *TIME Magazine for Kids*, March 27, 1998. http://www.pathfinder.com/TFK/archive/032798/cover.html.

Roberts, David. "Sieur de La Salle's Fateful Landfall." *Smithsonian* Magazine (April 1997).

Salmon, Emily and Edward D. Campbell, Jr., eds. *The Hornbook of Virginia History*. Richmond: The Library of Virginia, 1994.

Sante, Luc. *Low Life: Lures and Snares of Old New York*. New York: Farrar, Straus & Giroux, 1991.

Scott, Douglas D. and Melissa A. Connor. "Post-mortem at the Little Bighorn." *Natural History* (June 1986).

Scott, Douglas D. and Richard A. Fox, Jr. *Archaeological Insights into the Custer Battle: An Assessment of the 1984 Field Season*. Norman: University of Oklahoma Press, 1987.

Seccia, Patrick T. "Black Elk, Holy Man of the Lakota, Was 13 Years Old When He Took a Scalp at the Little Bighorn." *Wild West*, 11, no. 4 (December 1998).

Silberman, N. A. "Remembering Custer." *Archaeology*, 43, no. 2 (March/April 1990).

"Slum Lore," *Village Voice*, January 1, 1996. (Volume 1).

Srinivasan, Kalpana. "Political Intrigue May Have Been Fatal in Early Jamestown." seattletimes.com, March 11, 1998. http://www.seattle-times.com/news/nation-world/html/98/altjame_031198.html.

Stanton, Lucia. *Slavery at Monticello*. Charlottesville, Va.: Thomas Jefferson Memorial Foundation, 1996.

Tate, Thad W., and David L. Ammerman, eds., *The Chesapeake in the Seventeenth Century*. New York: W. W. Norton & Company, 1980.

Taylor, William O. *With Custer on the Little Bighorn.* New York: Viking Press, 1996.

Terrell, John Upton. *La Salle: The Life and Times of an Explorer.* New York: Weybright and Talley, 1968.

Texas State Historical Commission. "Cofferdam Fact Sheet." *The Medallion,* nd.

———. "Discovery of La Salle Shipwreck Hailed as Greatest Find in Decades." *The Medallion,* nd.

———. "Fate of the Belle." *The Medallion,* nd.

———. "La Salle Shipwreck Artifacts Exhibit Fact Sheet." *The Medallion,* nd.

Ward, A. "The Little Bighorn." *American Heritage,* 43, no.2 (April 1992).

Welch, James with Paul Stekler. *Killing Custer: The Battle of the Little Bighorn and the Fate of the Plains Indians.* New York: W. W. Norton & Company, 1994.

Wertime, Richard A. "The Landscape Genius." *Archaeology* (May/June 1993).

Wheat, Pam. "The *Belle*: A Gift from Louis XIV." *Journeys: A Newsletter for Educators,* 1, no.1. Austin: Texas State Historical Commission, 1996.

Wood, Ken. "Sifting Through History for Real Jamestown Story." SunNews.com, March 25, 1999. http://www.sunnews.com/news/newsmaker/nm99/newsmakr/032599.html.

Wright, Louis B. *A Voyage to Virginia in 1609: Two Narratives.* Charlottesville, Va.: Published for the Association for the Preservation of Virginia Antiquities, by the University Press of Virginia, 1964.

Yamin, Rebecca. "New York's Mythic Slum." *Archaeology* (March/April 1997).

Related Reading

Books

Aston, Mick and Tim Taylor. *The Atlas of Archaeology.* New York: DK Publishing, 1998.

Avi-Yonah, Michael. *Dig This!: How Archaeologists Uncover Our Past.* Minneapolis, Minn.: Runestone Press, 1993.

Ballard, Robert D. *Finding the Titanic.* New York: Cartwheel Books, 1993.

Buell, Janet, *Ancient Horsemen of Siberia.* Brookfield, Conn.: Millbrook Press, 1998.

———. *Ice Maiden of the Andes.* Brookfield, Conn.: Millbrook Press, 1997.

Deem, James M. *Bodies from the Bog.* New York: Houghton Mifflin, 1998.

Dubowski, Cathy East and Mark Dubowski. *Ice Mummy: The Discovery of a 5,000 Year Old Man.* New York: Random House, 1998.

Griffey, Harriet. *Eyewitness Readers: The Secret of the Mummies.* New York: DK Publishers, 1998.

Hansen, Joyce and Gary McGowan. *Breaking Ground, Breaking Silence: The Story of New York's African Burial Ground.* New York: Henry Holt and Company, 1998.

McGowen, Tom. *Adventures in Archaeology.* New York: Twenty-First Century Books, 1997.

Reid, Struan. *The Children's Atlas of Lost Treasures.* Brookfield, Conn.: Millbrook Press, 1997.

Samford, Patricia and David L. Ribblett. *Archaeology for Young Explorers: Uncovering History at Colonial Williamsburg.* Williamsburg, Va.: Colonial Williamsburg Foundation, 1995.

Stetoff, Rebecca. *Finding the Lost Cities: Archaeology and Ancient Civilizations.* New York: Oxford University Press, 1997.

Sullivan, George. *Slave Ship.* New York: Cobblehill Press, 1994.

Trimble, Kelly. *Cat Mummies.* New York: Clarion Books, 1996.

Web Sites

Society of Historical Archaeologists: http://www.sha.org
Official site for the society provides information on historical archaeology and includes a number of suggested readings and information on current projects.

Five Points: http://r2.gsa.gov/fivept/fphome.html
Site provides a "tour" of the Five Points neighborhood and excavation project.

Jamestown: http://www.apva.org/ngex/jfort
From the APVA, this site provides a historical overview and current updates on the Jamestown Rediscovery Project.

Little Bighorn: http://www.custerbattle.com
A fascinating site that provides an overview of the archaeology and history of the Little Bighorn.

Midwest Archaeological Center: http://www.mwac.nps.gov
See actual site photos and learn more about the archaeology of the battle site from the Midwest Archaeological Center, whose teams carried out much of the work.

Little Bighorn Battlefield National Monument: http://www.nps.gov/libi/
From the National Park Service, the official site for the battleground park. Provides a history of the battle, educational activities, and park information.

Monticello: http://www.monticello.org
This web site from the Jefferson Memorial Foundation provides an overview of Monticello, including its history, educational activities, and tour information.

Texas Historical Commission (La Salle): http://www.thc.state.tx.us
Here the THC has provided information on all aspects of the La Belle *project. There are also a number of articles that provide information on La Salle and his time, as well as educational activities.*

Index